You're Just a Girl

A MEMOIR

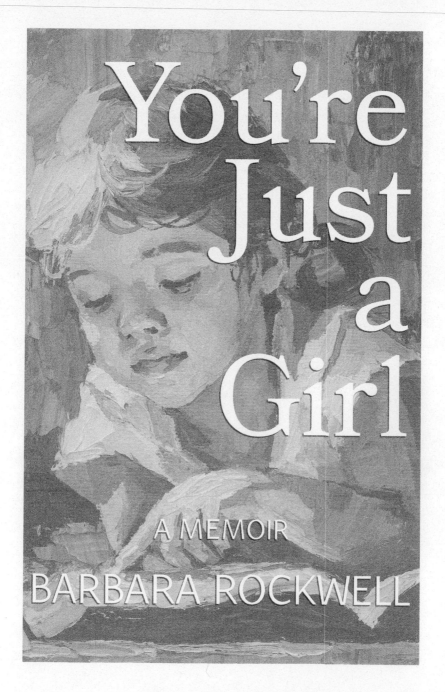

You're Just a Girl

A MEMOIR

BARBARA ROCKWELL

Desert Wind Press

The events and conversations in this book have been set down to the best of the author's ability, although some names and details have been changed to protect the privacy of individuals.

Cover and Book Design by Robert Brent Gardner
Photos provided by Barbara Rockwell and Jeremy Kershaw

Independently published by Desert Wind Press

ISBN 978-1-956271-10-2 (print softcover)

Acknowledgments

I'm grateful to Robert Brent Gardner of Desert Wind Press for the production of this book, including the format for the text and cover design. I appreciate his patience and advice in making this book attractive and readable.

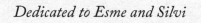

Dedicated to Esme and Silvi

Gilpin

CHAPTER 1

My Roots

*L*ike many people when they retire and have time on their hands, I did some research on the Gilpin family, my mother's side of our family. The Gilpins were Quakers and the Quakers keep very good records. I didn't have much luck with my father's side, the Rahners. All I know is that they came from Alsace Lorraine in Germany and that my great grandfather, Adolf Rahner, was a draft dodger from the Franco Prussian war. He emigrated to Philadelphia in the 1870s and was a baker by profession. The Rahner name gained a lot of luster in the early 1960s when Karl Rahner was named chief theologian at Vatican II. That gained me a lot of points with the nuns at my high school. I soon lost interest in the genealogy project and moved on to something else for post-retirement entertainment.

Here's what I learned about my mom's side, the Gilpins, taken from The North American Philadelphia, Sunday, May 24, 1908, titled "The Philadelphia of Our Ancestors -- Old Philadelphia Families...LI... Gilpin" Conducted by Frank Willing Leach and Albert Cook Myers

"Joseph Gilpin, son of Thomas and Joan born April 1662 and died

September 9, 1741. Married Hannah Glover 12/23/1691 at Baghurst Meeting. Hannah died January 12, 1757 at 82 years old. Her uncle Wm. Lamboll gave her 200 acres, later increased to 425 acres in 1713. They came to New Castle in 1695 with Hannah (3) and Samuel (1).

They landed at New Castle-on-Delaware in 1695, according to the written account of Isaac Glover Gilpin, a grandson, and set on foot through the wilderness, for their farm, eighteen miles to the northern, in what was afterward known as Birmingham Township, Chester County.From the grandson's chronicle, we have these interesting items relating the early and later experiences of the emigrants, following the disembarkation at New Castle

"About ten or eleven miles distant from New Castle, night overtook them. In this situation they applied at the habitation of an early settler for shelter, which was refused them...Fortunately some of the natives lived near, into whose wigwams they were received and treated kindly; and they lodged there for their first night ashore in America...Next morning, being refreshed, they went on and arrived in Birmingham township, Chester county...

"They had at first to dig a cave in the earth and went into it, in which they lived for four or five years, and where two children were born. [Rachel & Ruth]...After Joseph Gilpin had resided in the cave for four or five years, he built a house and barn near the cave, but this was burnt, and then he built a frame house a few hundred yards to the westward, it was built two stories high 16 feet by 18 feet, a superb edifice for the time."

The above mentioned house was built about 1720, a brick addition being made in 1754. It is said to have been occupied by General Howe after the Battle of Brandywine. The original frame building was torn down in 1835, and replaced by a stone structure. The house, including the brick section erected in 1754, still stands. {See photo in Quaker Date Book (1961)} The grandson's narrative thus continues:

"There were a number of Indian wigwams on the farm of Joseph Gilpin, and the account we have is that they all lived together in perfect harmony...Joseph Gilpin's house was seldom clear of the Indians who frequently slept there, perhaps a dozen or more at a time-men, women and children, all peaceably and much friendship...The children of Joseph Gilpin give very pleasant and interesting accounts of their sports and games with Indian boys,-of their shooting with them for days at a time with bows and arrows.- there was no quarrelling or fighting."

Joseph Gilpin's hospitality was likewise extended in equal measure to all newly arrived emigrants, quite in contrast to his own reception the night after landing.

The grandson thus writes:

"As he was so well known there great numbers of families on coming over, came to his house, where they were kindly received and entertained week after week. As an evidence of this writer, who was an inmate of Joseph's family-knew that he killed upwards of 30 hogs and 7 or 8 Beeves in the fall season-and the meat was all duly and frugally consumed by the next harvest. Hannah Gilpin, was the best of housewives,-and superior to most in intellect and friendly conduct."

Thomas Chalkey, the celebrated Quaker preacher and traveler, born in 1675, and died in 1741, makes the following note in his journal in 1740:

"Lodged at the widow Gilpin's, whose husband, Joseph Gilpin, was lately deceased; there was true Christian Love and Friendship between us for above fifty years. When first I saw Joseph in Pennsylvania, he lived in a cave in the Earth, where we enjoyed each others Company in the Love and Fear of God. This friend had fifteen children, who he

lived to see brought up to the States of Men and Women, and all but two married well and to his mind. "

As stated in Chalkley's journal, of the fifteen Gilpin children all but two had, prior to the father's death, in 1739, "married well and to his mind". As a matter of fact, these two, the youngest son (Joseph] and the youngest daughter, [Esther] married shortly after their father's decease. With the Gilpin family it was a remarkable case of longevity, only one of the fifteen children having died under the age of sixty years. At the time of Hannah's death in 1757, there were living twelve children, sixty-two grand children and nearly as many great-grand children, one hundred and thirty three living descendants in all!" Here in a nutshell is the early history of my ancestors, the Gilpins, an ancient family originating in Normandy. One of the de Guylpens came with William the Conqueror to England in 1066. The name was eventually anglicized to Gilpin. In 1206 King John gave Richard del Guylpyn, the first documented Gilpin, the manor of Kentmere Hall in the Lake District of England for killing a huge wild boar that had been terrorizing the area for too long. The Gilpin crest features a giant hog rampant with tusks and "gules."

My Aunt Ginny Gilpin visited Kentmere Hall a dozen years ago and reported that the old stone walls are now the foundation of a barn for cows and pigs. But back to 1206 and then fast forward 450 years to the bloody English Civil Wars of the mid 1600s. Joseph Gilpin's father was so sickened by the fighting of brother against neighbor that he became a member of a new pacifist sect, the Friends aka the Quakers. The peace-loving Quakers were a threat to the remorseless Puritans who jailed them and confiscated their land. Joseph's parents Thomas and Joan were severely persecuted for their Quaker faith. Thomas was jailed and they lost everything, "even the crops in the fields of their farm." They were "'left with not a pot in which to boil their food."

This sets the stage for the story of the first American Gilpins, the emigrants Joseph and Hannah Glover Gilpin who came to Pennsylvania in 1695 in a little wooden sailing ship and went on to raise a tremendous family and to leave a legacy of hospitality and friendship with other immigrants and with the Lenape natives. These are the Gilpins I'm interested in writing about, Hannah and Joseph and through them, my grandparents, Ernie and Mary Gilpin. I am especially interested in the first Gilpin's life-long friendship with the Lenape people whom I think were the bedrock of the family's success in their new home.

I am a direct descendant of Hannah & Joseph through my grandfather Ernie Gilpin. I lived with him and my grandmother Mary when I was four and five and was very fond of them. They had one of the nicest marriages I've ever seen. He would come up behind her at the stove and nuzzle her neck. She would giggle and say "Get away with ya you article" spoofing a faint brogue copied from her mother The Duchess straight off the boat from Cork. We kids loved to see this. I called them Gammy and Gampy, names that my mother told me I made up and that stuck somehow with the rest of the family. Gampy was different from the rest of the family who were all of German and Irish stock. He had cornflower blue eyes and a calm quiet manner. No one ever saw him lose his temper. He might puff very rapidly on his pipe when stressed but that was it for drama. The Gilpins come from the north of England where the people are noted for 'not jumping about and shouting.' Everyone respected Gampy. He had gravitas. He was a workingman but a refined man who liked to read the National Geographic to us kids after dinner in the backyard in the summer, slapping mosquitoes all the while. He liked to follow the stock market although he did not invest in it as far as I know. I remember shyly asking him what the columns of numbers meant. He lifted me up to sit next to him and explained it to me in a way that made perfect sense to a five-year old.

He and Gammy had seven children and never much money. During the Depression they lived in a rented colonial-era house in New Jersey with orchards, gardens, massive rose bushes and a large flock of chickens so they were never hungry. My grandmother was a magical cook to my young palate. My father loved her cooking too, good plain American food. He would boast that she could make a gallon of delicious gravy from a teaspoon of drippings. Ernie taught Mary to make the gravy when they were first married and he would eat it on his pancakes for breakfast. We never ate exotic things like rice and spaghetti but we did have creamed dandelion greens in spring. Gammy would send us kids out onto the back lawn to pick it before dinner.

Back to the old house they lived in during the Depression that was held together with wooden pegs, not a single nail, no indoor plumbing or heating. Each room had a fireplace and the children were sent to bed in winter with a hot brick wrapped in a towel to warm their bed. In summer, the kids were bathed in a horse trough in the backyard. It sounded idyllic to an old back-to-the-earther like me but my mother did not remember it that way. She remembered wearing odd clothes made from worn-out adult dresses cut down to size by her grandmother and being afraid of attack from Gampy's prize rooster when she went into the chicken coop to collect eggs. She did admit the peaches and grapes in summer were heavenly, eaten while lying in the long grass in the orchard. I never saw the house; it gave way to an expanding gravel pit sometime in the 1950s.

This nostalgic connection to an old house made me think of another old colonial house, Shipley Farm in Secane, Pennsylvania. where my sister and I babysat during the early 1960s. It was a fascinating place built in stages over three centuries. There was a small library near the kitchen full of old books inscribed in copperplate script "Nicholas Shipley." It was an elegant three-storey house with all the rooms a step up or a step down. My sister Pat and I were always a little spooked in the house at night, sensing a ghost around every corner. The house was redolent with vibes from the generations of people who lived there.

During my teens Aunt Ginny showed me an article in a series on founding families that was being run by the Philadelphia Inquirer. I read the story of the first Gilpins and how they lived in a cave for five years when they first landed in America and how their children and grandchildren went on to become one of the founding families of Philadelphia. I wondered if there was a connection between the Shipleys and the Gilpins since both families were Quaker and they lived near one another in an age when the population was small and the marriage opportunities were probably pretty slim. A little research on the internet revealed that Shipleys did indeed marry Gilpins and that the last of the Indians who had a home in Delaware County was "Indian Nelly," who had her cabin in Springfield near the line of the Shipley farm, residing there as late as 1810. I found a wealth of information about the 15 Gilpin children, who they married and the names of their children. I found out that Colonel George Gilpin was an aide to George Washington, a personal friend after the war and a pallbearer at his funeral. Another great great aunt married a Washington. During the Revolutionary War, General Howe, the British commander took over the Gilpin homestead for his headquarters for a week after Washington's defeat in the Battle of Brandywine. The Marquis de Lafayette was taken to Gideon Gilpin's farmhouse when he was wounded in the battle. When Lafayette returned to visit the battlefield in 1825, he stopped in to visit his old host Gideon who was then on his death bed. Gideon's farm was plundered by the British after the battle and the family was impoverished for a time. The British took 14 milk cows, one yoke of oxen, 48 sheep, 28 pigs, 12 tons of hay, 230 bushels of wheat, 50 pounds of bacon, one history book and one gun from what had been a prosperous farm. Gideon turned his house into a tavern for a time to support his family much to the disapproval of the Quakers.

I had no idea until I read this that our family had such a colorful past.

In our teen years, my dad took my sister and me to Brandywine, not far from our home in Morton to see these houses. I remember sitting by Brandywine Creek and dreaming of spending summer days on the shady banks of that lazy brown river. I have always had a sense of longing or nostalgia for that lost time, primeval forests full of birdsong, fresh clear water teeming with life. When I grew up the rivers and creeks were polluted, dead and dangerous. We lived a block away from Darby Creek, a small river that flows into the Delaware River about 20 miles from the Brandywine Creek. I was warned over and over not to swim in Darby Creek and kids were known to get sick from it. The nearby city of Chester was an industrial area, poor and desolate and the outskirts of Philadelphia 20 miles on the other side of us were the same dying eyesore. What was supposed to be a bird refuge bordering on Darby Creek was a dumping ground for industry (in recent years Darby Creek has been restored; shad and bass are back and thriving after several dams were torn down). I was aware at a very young age that I lived in a polluted world. Perhaps it was a coincidence but both my sister and I came down with Graves Disease when we were in our late 20s. Graves is an autoimmune disease of the thyroid that can be brought about by environmental contamination.

Even as a five year old, I dreamed of the pristine world that the first Gilpins came to at the Brandywine. It was long before the Industrial Revolution, the land was thickly wooded with old growth forest and full of wildlife, the air and the water were pure.

When I was old enough at 19, I went to Bermuda on vacation with girlfriends, managed to get a job and never came back. Bermuda was the first clean environment I ever lived in and I loved it. There was no going back but I've always held dear those early fantasies of a beautiful unspoiled place.

When I was four I had a strange 'vision' that I've never forgotten. I was standing alone in my grandmother's kitchen doing nothing in particular when everything shifted and I was in another kitchen, another place that was utterly strange but wonderful. It probably only lasted seconds, I don't know. The atmosphere was something I can't describe in words, it was a flavor of another time. I wanted to stay there. It was like dreaming while wide awake. I didn't know what to make of this experience and still don't but I know it sharpened my feelings of nostalgia and loss.

In my early twenties I lived for two years in Jackson Hole, Wyoming in a tiny cabin with no running water and a cook stove for heat. For some reason I was driven to find out how little I could live on and be happy. I found out I could be content with very little in the way of material goods and that has helped me understand and appreciate the life of the first Gilpins

The Gilpin family stories I grew up with were these: a grandmother was a cook in a logging camp on the Ohio frontier got caught in a big forest fire and all the animals went into the river with her to save themselves; my great grandfather, Gampy's father Elijah Beebe Gilpin, at the age of two was present at the hanging of John Brown at Harper's Ferry in 1859 (what a strange coincidence that I would meet and marry John Brown's great great nephew almost 115 years later.) Gampy told us about his neighborhood in Philadelphia during the Spanish Flu epidemic of 1918, the bodies stacked up on the sidewalk for the cart to take away and how he saw the Hindenberg crash in New Jersey in 1937.

These stories were word of mouth passed down and there was no further detail. Just the bare bones and no way to find out anything more. The internet did not exist and we were not sophisticated enough to use the libraries. I went back to the internet after I discovered the Shipley/

Gilpin connection and found excerpts of Isaac Glover Gilpin's journal entries of the 1750s about his grandparents, Joseph and Hannah Gilpin. My imagination was captured.

Thanks to Isaac Gilpin - god bless him that he wrote it down. Here's what he wrote and where it took me:

"They landed at New Castle-on-Delaware in 1695 and set on foot through the wilderness, for their farm, eighteen miles to the northern, in what was afterward known as Birmingham Township, Chester County."

Joseph Gilpin was a weaver aged 28 and Hannah Glover a 23 year old spinster when they married in 1691at Friends Meeting Place in Baghurst, Alton, Southampton, England. A Quaker wedding is a modest affair like everything else Quaker. The wedding guests gather in silent meeting and the couple make promises to one another that are short and simple. Since there is no clergy, the couple marry one another in the presence of God.

When they undertook the grand and great adventure of coming to the new world in 1695 they were practically middle-aged for the time at 32 and 27 and had two children, three-year old Hannah and one-year old Samuel. Both of Hannah's parents were dead when they set off for America which must have avoided a lot of anguish. Joseph's father was dead but his mother lived on until 1700. It's hard to imagine now but when children left parents to relocate in those days, they were usually never seen again. The Irish held The American Wake.

The Society of Friends, or Quakers had been persecuted and imprisoned for over forty years until 1689 when the Toleration Act was passed. The passage of this law probably offered cold comfort to Joseph and Hannah after what they had experienced and seen their parents experience. How could they be sure that the persecution would not return? It was time to leave England and Hannah's gift of land in

Pennsylvania was the way out.

I've always been attracted to the Quaker faith with its belief in the "Inner Light." They believe that an individual can have a direct experience with God without the intervention of clergy. The Quakers never tried to force the Lenape to adopt their beliefs. In contrast to other Christian sects, Quakers respected the beliefs of the Indians and did not hold themselves superior. Services are simple, sitting in meditation and speaking only if inspired to do so. I attended a Quaker meeting years ago in Tucson and no one spoke until someone got up to read a letter from a young nephew serving in Viet Nam. Then he sat down and silent meditation continued. This was a revelation for me having been raised Catholic with all its medieval pomp and incense. Quakers are opposed to war and were among the first to oppose slavery and to free their slaves if they held them by 1780. The third-born of the Gilpin daughters, Rachel, had a home in Delaware that was a stop on the underground railroad. The same for my husband Dave's family, the Browns, who had an underground railroad stop in Hudson on the Ohio River. They also believed in the equality of women. I was a second-class citizen in the Catholic faith but not the Quaker, another thing I love about them. They were the first to treat the mentally ill and prisoners in a humane manner. And for these Christ-like ways Quaker women who dared to preach in New England were executed by the Puritans in the mid-1600s.

After witnessing the persecution of his parents, Joseph saw their chance for a new life when Hannah's uncle gave her 200 acres as a wedding present (later increased to 625 acres in 1713). Hannah's uncle Wm. Lamboll purchased the 625 acres from William Penn. At that time Penn was the largest private land owner in the world, having been given a very generous grant of 45,000 acres west of New Jersey and north of Maryland by King Charles II in 1680 in return for a debt owed to his father the Admiral. Penn first visited Pennsylvania (Penn's Woods) in 1682 and the next year entered into a peace treaty with Lenape chiefs under a giant elm tree in what is now Kensington in Philadelphia and paid them fairly for the land. The treaty was depicted in a famous painting by Benjamin West, a Gilpin cousin, in 1771. Penn became a real estate entrepreneur, advertising throughout Europe the sale of land with the promise of religious freedom. Quakers, Amish, Mennonites, High-Germans, Huguenots, among other persecuted groups bought land and the settlers came sailing over to the new world utopia. How could Penn go wrong with such a windfall? He did - dying penniless after heedlessly signing a document for his larcenous business manager whose widow later claimed title to Penn's lands. She didn't get to keep her claim but Penn did land in debtor's prison for a while. Despite his bad management, he did succeed in establishing a colony where "all Persons are equal under God." Pennsylvania was a "Holy Experiment." This all fell apart after Penn's death when his two rotten sons cheated the Lenape out of their land in the infamous Walking Purchase.

Pennsylvania had 18,000 immigrants in 1699, four years after Joseph and Hannah arrived and they were concentrated along the coast since western Pennsylvania was then a vast wilderness. Philadelphia had 3,000 of that number. Here's what the founder of the first German settlement in Pennsylvania, Germantown, Francis Daniel Pastorius had to say in 1683: "It is truly a matter for amazement how quickly, by the blessing of God, it advances, and from day to day grows perceptibly." Not so sure it was a blessing, but today Pennsylvania's population is around 12 million.

There is no record I could find but Hannah and Joseph probably sailed from the Isle of Wight off Southampton as did William Penn on his second visit in 1699 (he lived in Pennsylvania for only four years). One account says that their companions on the voyage were the Morris and Coats families of Philadelphia. Penn sailed with his family on the

Canterbury and had an exciting encounter with pirates on the way over. Who knows what Hannah and Joseph's voyage was like although we can be pretty sure it was unpleasant at best. It required a great deal of courage since it was such a dangerous undertaking -- and they were travelling with children, three-year old Hannah and one-year old Samuel.

I would like to imagine a happier scenario: a summer sea, dolphins following the ship, a night sky full of stars, the little family sleeping in the sweet air on deck after a supper of fish caught over the side that day, sailors dancing to the hornpipe on the foredeck under a full moon...

Here's the worst case scenario from Gottlieb Mittelberger who emigrated in 1750:

"...during the voyage there is on board these ships terrible misery, stench, fumes, horror, vomiting, many kinds of seasickness, fever, dysentery, headache, heat, constipation, boils, scurvy, cancer, mouth rot, and the like, all of which come from old and sharply-salted food and meat, also from very bad and foul water, so that many die miserably."

Hannah and Joseph travelled to America 55 years before this big migration and perhaps their little wooden ship was not so crowded. I was surprised again to discover how busy the Atlantic was - there were around 500 transatlantic crossings each year, many of them slave ships. Here's an excerpt from the story of the Brownell family crossing:

"When a passenger left London he could not say within many weeks how long he was to be on board the ship taking him to America. The ships were slow sailers, although they could go as fast as eight miles an hour when there was a fair wind and a smooth sea. But never was this rate kept up for even twenty-four hours.

Often four or five miles was all there was to show for a whole day. There were even times when they were further from their destination at the end of twenty-four hours than at the beginning. The length of the voyage could vary from 47 to 138 days. Sometimes ships that left London at the same time might arrive in America as much as eight or nine weeks apart.

Conditions on board were far from ideal, even for those times. Most ships were over-crowded with passengers, and private cabins were available only to the ship's captain and a very few, if any, important passengers. All the others slept on the floor on the deck below the main deck.

There was very little light or air. Often water would pour in through cracks and joints, drenching the passengers and their belongings. There were no bathrooms on board. If you wanted to wash, you had to wash in salty water from the sea. Most likely you would wear the same clothes for the entire voyage.

Meals usually consisted of salt horse (salted beef, pork or fish) and hardtack (a hard, dry biscuit). There were dried peas and beans, cheese and butter. Weather permitting, food was cooked over charcoal fires in metal boxes called braziers. But it was often too dangerous to have a fire and so the food was eaten cold. Food became infested with bugs, the biscuits got too hard to eat, the cheese got moldy, butter turned bad and even the beer began to go sour by the end of the voyage.

A large amount of water was taken on board, but after standing in barrels for a while, it was neither pleasant nor safe to drink. Everyone, even the children, drank beer instead.

Storms were a great danger, and the Atlantic had many, especially in the fall and winter. The tossing and rolling of these small ships in even a minor storm caused most of the passengers, many of whom had never been on a ship before, to become seasick. A major storm could easily capsize ships of this size or cause them to break apart.

Sickness, other than seasickness, was also a major problem. Even a *minor illness could quickly spread among passengers and crew alike. Serious illnesses, often called ship's fever, killed many passengers. On some voyages as many as half the passengers died before they reached their final destination.*

The prospect of this long, dangerous and unpleasant voyage was not made more tolerable by the conditions passengers faced upon arrival in America. There were no hotels in which to stay, no restaurants in which to eat, nor often even relatives or friends to greet them."

This was certainly true for the Gilpins. There was no one there to greet them. The intense fragrance of land that can be smelled out to sea did greet them and it must have been intoxicating. We can only imagine their joy and relief at arriving safely.

New Castle was a settlement at the head of the Delaware Bay founded in 1651 by Peter Stuyvesant of the Dutch West India Company. It was fought over by the Dutch and the Swedes, then by the English and the Dutch for years. The English finally prevailed and New Castle was given to William Penn who landed there for the first time in 1682. It was the seat of colonial government until Penn moved it to Philadelphia in the early 1700s much to the relief of the Dutch, Swedish and English residents who were not happy with the conservative Quaker ways. The Old Gilpin House on Delaware St is one of town's oldest buildings . It was built as the town's hotel/tavern and served as such until Prohibition in 1920, but when Hannah and Joseph landed it did not yet exist. They gathered their belongings, probably bought some supplies like cornmeal and lard, and with their two children, set off on foot.

Their grandson Isaac goes on:

"About ten or eleven miles distant from New Castle, night overtook them. In this situation they applied at the habitation of an early settler for shelter, which was refused them...Fortunately some of the natives

lived near, into whose wigwams they were received and treated kindly;
and they lodged there for their first night ashore in America...Next
morning, being refreshed, they went on and arrived in Birmingham
township, Chester county..."

Poor Hannah and Joseph, they must have been so tired and hungry, no doubt carrying the children most of the way. This wretched "early settler" was probably one of the Dutch or Swedes who did not like the Quakers, but to refuse food and shelter was an outrageous violation of the biblical laws of hospitality for that time. The 'natives,' meaning the Lenape who took them in made lasting lifelong ties of goodwill with Hannah and Joseph. One account claims that the natives accompanied the young family to their land and helped them settle in. Chadds Ford, Delaware County as Birmingham township, Chester County is now known since 1996, is a beautiful country of gently rolling hills, woods and streams. It is hot and humid in the summer with usually mild winters, almost a subtropical climate.

Isaac Gilpin continues:

"They had at first to dig a cave in the earth and went into it, in which
they lived for four or five years, and where two children were born.
[Rachel & Ruth]...After Joseph Gilpin had resided in the cave for four
or five years, he built a house and barn near the cave, but this was burnt,
and then he built a frame house a few hundred yards to the westward,
it was built two stories high 16 feet by 18 feet, a superb edifice for the
time."

The cave was dug under a large rock outcropping and then used as a dump after the house was built. To this day, 18th century artifacts turn up. From the Philadelphia of Our Ancestors published in 1908 by Frank Willing Leach: "The above mentioned house was built about 1720, a brick addition being made in 1754. It is said to have been occupied by General Howe after the Battle of Brandywine. The original frame building was torn down in 1835, and replaced by a stone structure. The house, including the brick section erected in 1754, still stands."

This was the house my dad took my sister Pat and me to see when we were young teenagers in the early 1960s. We did not see the cave. Who has children in a cave and moves forward in friendship and love with neighbors? They were living literally on the earth just like the Lenape on whose land they had settled. I wonder if there was ever a conversation or any debate about who "owned" the land. Ownership and title was a foreign concept to the Indians who believed that we all simply share the land given to us by the Creator. The women of a clan had rights to their own fields and the men to certain hunting areas but there was no concept of title. This innocence would of course be the undoing of the Lenape....but not as long as Hannah and Joseph Gilpin were alive.

We know the natives who guided the family to their farm advised the Gilpins to build near a spring so they would have a constant water source. I'm sure the Lenape gave them all kinds of generous advice and survival skills in their new home. They knew how to thrive off the land. Perhaps they shared their seeds or maybe Hannah and Joseph brought their own supply, who knows, there's no record, but plenty is known of Lenape agriculture. They planted two kinds of corn, and when the corn was up they planted beans at the base to grow up the cornstalk for support. Then they planted squash to shade the ground and crowd out any weeds. For sweetening, they harvested 'tree sugar' from maple trees and boiled it down into brown loaves for storage through the winter. A great treat was wild honey harvested in the woods. They harvested clams and oysters and smoked them for the winter. They hunted venison and there was plenty of fish which they flayed and pinned to a plank to cook next to the fire. They used bear grease for cooking and many other purposes. In late summer they picked berries of all kinds for drying and eating fresh. Hannah and Joseph were fortunate to have Lenape friends show them the way.

Here's what Pastorius said about the Lenni Lenape or Delaware Indians in 1683, the time of Penn's first visit: "… the savages, they are, in general, strong, agile, and supple people, with blackish bodies; they went about naked at first and wore only a cloth about the loins. Now they are beginning to wear shirts. They have, usually, coal-black hair, shave the head, smear the same with grease, and allow a long lock to grow on the right side. They also besmear the children with grease and let them creep about in the heat of the sun, so that they become the color of a nut, although they were at first white enough by Nature." I'll bet the 'grease' Pastorius refers to was an herbal concoction meant to repel biting insects and protect against the sun's rays. Pennsylvania is notoriously buggy in the summer and I'm sure the canny Lenape knew just which crushed herbs to mix with bear grease to repel the mosquitoes and black flies. Of course this must have looked bizarre to the Europeans who at that point, were still learning about their new environment.

Pastorius writes: "The trade between the savages and the Christians is in fish, birds, deer-skins, and all sorts of peltry such as beaver, otter, fox, etc. Sometimes they barter for drink, sometimes they sell for their native money, which is only oblong corals, ground out of sea-mussels, sometimes white and sometimes light brown, and fastened on strings. They know how to string this coral-money in a very artistic way, and they wear it in the place of gold chains. Their king wears a crown or hood of it. Twelve of the brown are worth as much as twenty-four of the white pieces, which are equal to a silver penny of Franckfurt [Germany]. They take their own money far more readily than silver coin because they have often been cheated with the latter."

The grandson Isaac's narrative goes on:

"There were a number of Indian wigwams on the farm of Joseph

Gilpin, and the account we have is that they all lived together in perfect harmony...Joseph Gilpin's house was seldom clear of the Indians who frequently slept there, perhaps a dozen or more at a time-men, women and children, all peaceably and much friendship...The children of Joseph Gilpin give very pleasant and interesting accounts of their sports and games with Indian boys,-of their shooting with them for days at a time with bows and arrows.- there was no quarrelling or fighting."

It sounds like the Gilpins went native, but not really. Although they had wigwams on their farm, they did not live in one. According to Isaac Gilpin, the Indians instead slept in their house. Joseph and Hannah were staunch Quakers and Hannah especially was a very active member of the Concord meeting for all her life. The Concord Meeting House was organized before 1697, just a few years after Hannah and Joseph settled nearby. The meeting location was leased from John Mendenhall for "one peppercorn yearly forever." A log building was erected in 1710, although the community probably met at one another's homes before there was an official meeting house.

Joseph and Hannah were well known for their hospitality as the years went by. Their grandson writes:

"As he was so well known there great numbers of families on coming over, came to his house, where they were kindly received and entertained week after week. As an evidence of this writer, who was an inmate of Joseph's family-knew that he killed upwards of 30 hogs and 7 or 8 Beeves in the fall season-and the meat was all duly and frugally consumed by the next harvest. Hannah Gilpin, was the best of housewives,-and superior to most in intellect and friendly conduct."

Thomas Chalkley, the well-known Quaker preacher, a contemporary of Hannah and Joseph, noted in his journal in 1740, just a year before his death:

"Lodged at the widow Gilpin's, whose husband, Joseph Gilpin, was lately deceased; there was true Christian Love and Friendship between us for above fifty years. When first I saw Joseph in Pennsylvania, he lived in a cave in the Earth, where we enjoyed each others' Company in the Love and Fear of God. This friend had fifteen children, who he lived to see brought up to the States of Men and Women, and all but two married well and to his mind."

I was struck reading this account and others from that time that Hannah's role as mother and partner to Joseph is not mentioned. You would think Joseph bore and raised these children all on his own! This does not square with the Quaker belief that men and women are equal. Perhaps it was just the literary convention of the time. Quaker women were considered 'spiritual equals.' Looks like this 'equality' didn't extend to the material world.

These two children, the youngest son Joseph, and the youngest daughter Esther married shortly after their father's death. When I was growing up, it was often noted that Gampy's side of the family were long lived and this trait seems to go all the way back to Hannah and Joseph's family. When my sister and I were little, Gampy's mother, my great-grandmother Mary Elizabeth Gilpin (nee Stanley) lived with us for a time. Almost blind, she spent her days in a darkened room in a rocking chair. We kids were told to leave her alone, and we were intimidated but curious. We would sneak in and try to be quiet as mice rummaging in her closet. I still remember the strange smells of her things in that closet. I couldn't appreciate this at the time of course, but she was born in 1861 at the beginning of the Civil War. She died in 1956.

After bearing and raising 15 children, Hannah lived to the awesome age for that time of 82. It was reported that at the time of her death in 1757, there were twelve children living, sixty two grandchildren and nearly as many great-grandchildren, one hundred and thirty three living descendants in all! Only one of the 15 children died under the age of sixty. In contrast, Chalkley, who was constantly traveling away from his family, lost all of his ten children by two wives. They may have survived if he had stayed home to help his wife with the family. He left her alone in Philadelphia to run his business while he went on the road visiting and enjoying other Friends' hospitality. He even visited far flung places like Barbados and Bermuda.

It was usual in those days to lose children to disease so it's amazing that the Gilpins did not lose even one child. I'm sure their close association with the Lenape had everything to do with that extraordinary record. The Lenape were skilled in the use of medicinal herbs and medicine. It's been recorded that the early pioneers sought out Indian medicine when needed over what they could get from the white physician.

Dr. Gladys Tantaquidgeon (who lived to the age of 106) was a Mohegan Tribal medicine woman who wrote a book on the folk medicine of the Delaware titled "A Study of Delaware Indian Medicine Practice and Folk Beliefs." She documented dozens of herbs, roots and tree bark that were used alone or in combination to cure everything from toothache to arthritis to diabetes. The Delaware believed then as we do now that a pure diet and clean water is the basis for good health. Women were attended by a midwife and women over thirty giving birth, like Hannah, were given a 'special medicine' to shorten the period of labor. During the pregnancy, women drank tonics like raspberry leaf tea and after the birth, women were given a tea of Butterfly Weed (Asclepias tuberosa) or Rattlesnake Plantain (Epipactis pubescens). Bark from the Black Haw (Viburnum prunifolium) was combined with the leaves of bloodroot or wild plum to make a tonic to strengthen the female organs. The Indians had a much lower birth rate than the white pioneers, having a child only every three to four years. One of the herbal concoctions is described as 'bringing on the menses,' perhaps an early version of the morning after pill? Hannah was in good hands with these women. I think we can credit them with her extraordinary success in giving birth to 15 healthy babies and then raising them to adulthood without losing one to disease. You have to wonder what the natives thought of the prolific Gilpins. Did they see it as a threat? Of course it was because so many children and their children put pressure on the land and resources.

Hannah probably didn't know it at the time, at least at first, but she had a special affinity with the Lenape women as a Quaker woman. Both groups believed in the spiritual equality of women and men. The Lenape are a matrilineal and matrilocal society meaning the child belongs to the mother's clan and their closest male relative is not the father but the mother's brother, their uncle. When a Lenape couple married, they lived with the bride's family and enjoyed all the support from her mother and sisters. The woman owned her own house and its furnishings. She owned the crops she raised in her garden and even the meat and skins that her man brought in. There was a lot of confusion around this with the Europeans who had never encountered this social arrangement before and whose women had no rights whatsoever. European women were chattel whereas the Lenape woman was an equal.

Although the women had a strong voice in tribal affairs, there was a division of labor that is pretty traditional: the women did the farming and food storage and preparation, the men did the heavy work clearing the field, cutting wood and hunting for meat. They made beautiful clothes from skins and turkey feathers, beaded and beribboned. It's recorded that the settlers were amazed at their skills in producing this clothing.

The Lenape first line of defense against illness was the sweat lodge. There were special rituals used by the "sweat doctor" to cure illnesses. They were a very clean people. Men and women had their own separate sweat lodges which they used once or twice a week followed by a plunge. I wonder if the Lenape who led Hannah and Joseph to their new home also introduced them to the sweat lodge. I'm sure they needed it after their long voyage across the Atlantic and long walk to their new home. We can only wonder at how far the Gilpins went in adopting the lifeways of their new friends.

This is from the official history of the Nanticoke Lenni-Lenape written by modern tribal members: "The peace loving Lenni-Lenape are called the "grandfathers" or "ancient ones" by many other tribes and are considered to be among the most ancient of the Northeastern Nations, spawning many of the tribes along the northeastern seaboard. We were known as warriors and diplomats, often keeping the peace and mediating disputes between our neighboring Native Nations and were admired by European colonist for our hospitality and mediation skills." It's no surprise that the peace-loving Lenape and the peace-loving Quaker Gilpins got along so well.

Hannah and Joseph settled in, Joseph busy with clearing the land to feed his growing family. Wouldn't it be lovely to have a journal of their first years on the Brandywine. All we have is the journal entry of their grandson Isaac and Thomas Chalkley.

Like the nursery rhyme about the old lady who lived in a shoe and had so many children she didn't know what to do – how did Hannah and Joseph find room for so many children all one or two years apart? The Quaker Date Book of 1961 reports "After Joseph Gilpin had resided in the cave for four or five years, he built a house and barn near the cave, but this was burnt, and then he built a frame house a few hundred yards to the westward, it was built two stories high 16 feet by 18 feet, a superb edifice for the time.

Quaker archivist R. L. Cooke wrote:

"Architects and historians now believe that the frame part of this house, first section built, was Joseph's original dwelling. They consider it 'probably the oldest frame house in the Delaware Valley – one of the

few remaining examples of an English type frame house covered with clapboards, typical of the seventeenth century. – Most of the present clapboards are hand-split and shaved red oak.' It may have been enlarged by Joseph – (let us hope so, since he had fifteen children!) – and later by his son Joseph, Jr. and his grandson Gideon.

Gideon owned the place during the Battle of the Brandywine, when Lafayette was his overnight guest. The situation was probably arranged by Gideon's first cousin, Colonel George Gilpin, aide to Washington, who was disowned by Concord Meeting. Lafayette stopped again in 1824 and paid his respects to old Gideon.

And it is in Lafayette's honor, rather than the Gilpin family, that this house has been restored, suitably furnished. Historians now agree that this was Joseph's original home, right on the Baltimore Pike, originally called the Chester-to-Nottingham Road."

The last child, Esther, was born in 1718 and the larger house built in 1720 so the question remains: where did they all sleep? I imagine the original cabin was very much like the Morton Homestead on Darby Creek in Prospect Park. I grew up playing on the grounds of this old log cabin and knew it well. A high school friend's family were caretakers during the 1960s and we thoroughly explored the cabin. It was certainly not big enough to hold a family of 17 plus the dozen or so Indians that grandson Isaac reports sleeping over. They must have spent a lot of time outdoors and snuggled up together like kittens at night. The Morton Homestead is one of the oldest buildings in Pennsylvania built before the Gilpins arrived and was part of the Swedish settlement that predated the English by more than fifty years.

My aunt Doris Gilpin married and had five children with Melvin (Bus) Swanland of Tinicum whose family descended from these very early settlers. We didn't know any of this at the time… We were just regular families living our lives. Who knew that we were all descended from the very first immigrants from so long ago. I remember Tinicum as a tidal marsh, a swampy flat ugly place full of snapping turtles and mosquitoes and in later years, a very busy airport runway. My cousin Chuck Swanland, a year older than me, looked like a Swede with his large round head and blond hair. His parents Doris and Bus were one of the couples who lived with Gammy and Gampy after the war until they got on their feet. Since we lived under the same roof, we became true cousins known to one another like brother and sister for better or worse, mostly worse. He was the culprit behind shattered windows, broken toys, spilled spittoons, and burrs ground into hair. He was a mischievous and very bright boy who went on to become a linguist and an American school headmaster in Japan. There he died of cirrhosis of the liver, a common killer with the Scandinavians, who share that unfortunate alcohol genome with the Indians and the Irish. His parents Doris and Bus followed Gammy and Gampy out to Arizona in the late 1960s. They had received a large settlement from the railroad for an accident that put Bus in the hospital for a year. He came out with one leg six inches shorter than the other and a resolve to stop drinking.

After WWII my grandparents Ernie and Mary Gilpin had six of their seven children living with them for a while, three married couples with one or two babies plus the three youngest, George, Winnie and Virginia who were teens. The only other son Edwin (Eddie) was in the Air Force in Korea. My grandmother made a huge wonderful dinner every night for fifteen people after which Winnie and Ginnie did the dishes. This was what Hannah's life was like, cooking for a multitude every day with the help of her daughters. Gammy spent all of Sunday afternoon baking pies and pastry for the coming week. Remember what Hannah's grandson wrote about her: "Hannah Gilpin was the best of housewives, and superior to most in intellect and friendly conduct." I wish I could have known her. The usual reaction people have to hearing that woman had 15 children is negative, how awful it must have been for her. I have a different take on it. I had only one child but I remember my pregnancy as a wonderful interval in my life; I've never felt better physically and emotionally. I think that Hannah may have enjoyed being constantly pregnant with all those joyful hormones surging through her. The Lenape women knew how to space their babies three to four years apart and if Hannah wanted to do that herself she could have called on her Lenape women friends for help but she didn't.

Although my grandparents had all their children and grandchildren living with them for a time, their house had five bedrooms; it was not a tiny cabin. Joseph Gilpin spent the first four years clearing land to grow food for his growing family. Only then did he use the milled logs to build a house for his family. The best way to clear land was to girdle the trees – cut a swath around the bark which will kill the tree, then wait a year or so and the dried-out dead tree is easy to fell.

I wonder how much they were advised by their Lenape neighbors. They were skilled at growing the Three Sisters: corn, beans and squash using the old way of burning fish bones that were mixed with wood ashes and added to the corn hills as an offering to the Maize Spirit. The Indians would take time out to go to the Jersey or Maryland shore to feast on clams and crabs during the summer season with their Nanticoke cousins and to smoke a supply for the winter. I hope the Gilpins went too. It was a tradition with Ernie and Mary Gilpin to take the kids down to the Jersey shore and camp on the beach for a week or two in the summer. There are no records or diaries, other than the little bit that grandson Isaac wrote to tell us about their daily lives and relationships. He does tell us that the Gilpin children played with the Lenape children in the meadows around their place. I wonder how they communicated. Did the Gilpin kids learn Lenape and the Lenape kids learn English?

Isaac wrote:

The children of Joseph Gilpin give very pleasant and interesting accounts of their sports and games with Indian boys,–of their shooting with them for days at a time with bows and arrows.– there was no quarrelling or fighting.

What happened to all these Gilpin offspring after this idyllic childhood? We know that education was important to the Quakers and the Gilpin children surely received at least a basic education although there is no record.

Here is what I was able to find on the internet:

Hannah, born February 15, 1692 in Great Britain, died July 1746. She married William Seal in 1718. They settled on the Brandywine. Their children were Rachel, Joseph, Hannah, William, Joshua and Caleb.

Samuel, born June 7, 1694 in Great Britain, died December 7, 1767. He married Jane Parker of Philadelphia in 1722 and settled in Concord. Their children were Mary, Joseph, Thomas, Hannah, Samuel, Rachel and George. Thomas refused military service in the Continental Army and was exiled to Winchester, Virginia in 1777 and died in 1778 from a cold he picked up when out on a walk. His brother George was aide to General Washington and unsuccessfully tried to intercede for his brother to stop the exile. Thomas' two sons Thomas and Joshua had a paper mill near Wilmington and in 1817 introduced a new method of manufacturing paper of continuous length that made them wealthy.

Rachel, born February 12, 1695 in the cave, died May 20, 1776. She married Joshua Peirce in 1722. Their children were Joshua, Joseph and Caleb. They built a fine red brick house that is now owned by the du Pont family and is part of the world famous Longwood Gardens originally planted by her grandsons Joseph and Samuel Peirce. Their house later became a stop on the underground railway for slaves.

Ruth, born August 28, 1697 in the cave, died 1758. She married Joseph Mendenhall in 1718 and settled in Kennett. Chester County. Their children were Isaac, Hannah, Joseph, Benjamin, Ann, Stephen and Jesse. Their descendents in Chester County are numerous.

Lidia, born September 11, 1698, died October 2, 1750. She married William Dean in 1722 and settled on land next to her sister Hannah. Her children were Isaac, Caleb and Hannah and perhaps more. She became a minister among Friends and visited parts of New England, New Jersey and Maryland.

Thomas, born July 23, 1700, died October 25, 1766. He married Rebecca Mendenhall in 1726, Hannah Knowles in 1728, and Ann Caldwell in 1730. Cause of deaths were probably childbirth. He rented a mill in Concord known as Gilpin's Mill.

Ann, born July 11, 1702, died September 15, 1759. She married Joseph Miller in 1724 and had two children, Joseph and Isaac . She married Richard Hallett of Long Island in 1739, a Quaker preacher. They had three children: Thomas, Lydia and Israel.

Joseph, born October 21, 1704, died December 31, 1792. He married. Mary Caldwell in 1729 and moved from Birmingham to Wilmington in 1761. Their children were Ruth, Orpha, Vincent, Gideon, Israel, Betty, Joseph, Hannah, Mary and Thomas.

Sarah, born June 2, 1706, died June 7, 1783. She married Peter Cook in 1730 and settled in Chester County. Their children were Jesse, Joseph, Samuel, Hannah, Ann, Sarah, and Peter.

George, born February 16, 1708, died October 15, 1773. He married. Ruth Caldwell in 1736. In 1760 he married Sarah Woodward.

His children were George, Betty and Isaac.

Isaac, born March 23, 1709, died 1745. He married. Mary Painter in 1736. Their children were Hannah and two sons who died in childhood.

Moses, born March 8, 1711, date of death unknown. He married Anne Buffington in 1742 and settled in Birmingham.

Alice, born December 7, 1714, date of death unknown. She married Richard Eavenson in 1739.

Mary, born January 16, 1716, died April 17, 1806. She married Philip Taylor and settled nearby. Their children were John, Stephen, Philip, Lydia, Ruth, Phoebe, Mary, Rachel and Hannah.

Esther, born March 9, 1718, died January 10, 1795. She married Samuel Painter. Their children were James, Joseph, Samuel, George, Thomas, Hannah and Lydia. They were married for 54 years.

Among the grandchildren there were nine Hannahs, eight Josephs, four Thomases, four Samuels, three Lydias and three Georges. You have to wonder how they kept it all straight at family gatherings. I remember Gammy would always say "our George" or "our Elizabeth" so maybe that's how they did it. For the most part they all settled near their parents' farm after marriage. Thomas, son of Samuel, as we know was exiled to Virginia in 1777 when he refused military service. But remember, by that time there were 133 children, grandchildren and great grandchildren of Joseph and Hannah. Not only were they under pressure to betray their Quaker faith and join the Continental army but they were surely running out of space down on the farm. Some opted to head out West, in this case West Virginia through one of the most beautiful scenic valleys in America bordered by the Blue Ridge Mountains.

At least one of the grandsons took the Great Trading Path (also known as the Great Warrior Path and later the Great Wagon Path) through the Shenandoah Valley to West Virginia. He became the father of John Gilpin born in 1800 whose son was George Lawrence Gilpin born in 1831 whose son was Elijah Beebie Gilpin born in 1857 and who was Gampy's father. I have not been able to trace which grandson of Hannah and Joseph my line of Gilpins descended from, record keeping was poor to non-existent in that wild part of the country. It was probably a George. There has been a George in every generation. I know they settled in what is now Cottageville, West Virginia where three mills were located. I suspect they were in the milling business as other family members were back on the Brandywine. At some point the West Virginia Gilpins returned to Pennsylvania after Gampy's father Elijah married his mother, Mary Elizabeth Stanley in West Virginia and moved to the Tacony neighborhood of Philadelphia. My great grandfather Elijah Beebie Gilpin was born in West Virginia, in the Appalachians which has always been a poverty-stricken area and relocated to Tacony (from the Lenape word for "woods") a neighborhood eight miles from center city Philadelphia. The industrialist Disston built a saw and file manufacturing center there in 1872 that eventually employed 5,000 people and was called Saw Town. Elijah may have had Gilpin relatives who paved the way for him to come back to Pennsylvania after their exile of three generations. It's hard to know how much contact was maintained over the years but however it happened, Elijah landed up in Tacony where he became the father of Mamie, Elsie, Roy, Eva, Inez and my grandfather Ernest (no Hannahs and Josephs !). When I was growing up, Gampy worked at the Navy Yard in Philadelphia making saws and files so as often happens, the child walked in his father's footsteps. Gampy also had all the farming skills for raising chickens and a garden. I remember the fine knives and spatulas he made for Gammy's kitchen and his tool bench in the cellar had saws and tools he made himself.

It's estimated that the descendants of Hannah and Joseph Gilpin now number around 25,000. Some became wealthy landowners, the Who's Who of Pennsylvania, some lawyers, mayors, bankers and diplomats but most worked with their hands like Hannah and Joseph and my grandfather Ernie. Gilpins married other immigrants from all over Europe over thirteen generations and that has thoroughly diluted the Quaker influence. Apparently Gampy's family lost the Quaker faith after settling among the Bible thumpers of West Virginia. He grew up in a strict Christian fundamentalist family, and he wanted nothing to do with organized religion when he grew up. However he agreed to raise his children Catholic when he married my grandmother Mary, an Irish German Catholic. I know he admired the Quaker faith. He once said it was the only religion that made sense to him. He liked the concept of the Inner Light and tolerance for others. The Gilpins used to live in a small geographic area in Delaware County, Pennsylvania - with the exception of the Denver branch of the Gilpins. The famed photographer Laura Gilpin comes from this branch. The Gilpins that went to Virginia in exile in1777 eventually returned to Pennsylvania. Now the Gilpin descendants are scattered throughout the world.

Gammy & Gampy moved to Tucson, Arizona when Gampy retired in the mid 1960s. I think they wanted to escape the demands of their large family and spend their final years together in their snug little trailer house. Gampy died at 77 in his sleep. He knew he was going to die that night. He kissed Gammy and said "it's been a good life, Mary." Gammy held him in her arms until late the next morning when she called her daughter Doris who lived in Tucson to tell her that he had died. Gammy lived on another ten years, living with one daughter, Winnie and her family in Las Vegas then another daughter Elizabeth in New Jersey. She never stopped grieving for Gampy. She told me once that she was looking forward to joining him in heaven. I hope she did.

The Gilpins
(Top row from left) sister Pat, Aunt Ginny, Gammy, Uncle Ed, Aunt
Winnie, me.
(Bottom row from left) Dad, Uncle George and Gampy. Missing are Aunt
Elizabeth and Doris and their families.
Mom is taking the picture

CHAPTER 2

Some Family History

My mother was born Barbara Cecilia Gilpin in 1926 and grew up during the Great Depression. Her nickname in the family was Tibby. All but one of her five sisters had nicknames: Elizabeth, the oldest, was Id, Doris, the second, was Dink, and my mom the third, was Tib. The two youngest girls were Virginia or Ginny and Winifred, the baby, was Wee. I've often wondered why Ginny didn't have a cute nickname like the others….maybe she was the nicknamer…. There were two brothers in the mix as well, George and Edwin aka Our George and Eddy. The Gilpins are an old Quaker family who arrived on the Eastern shore from England in 1695. Every generation has had a George, probably because a grandson of the original American Gilpins was an aide de camp to George Washington and one of the pallbearers at his funeral. The Quakers kicked him out for joining the military but the name has remained popular through the generations. Despite this glorious footnote to the Gilpin family history, my grandparents were humble working people. They made it through the Depression on a rented farm in New Jersey where they raised chickens and vegetables. My mom described this farm – which was gobbled up by a gravel pit in the 1950s – as an old old house that was held together by wooden pegs, no nails. Each room had a fireplace for heat. She said when the kids went to bed in the winter, my grandmother, Gammy, would put hot water bottles under the covers at their feet. There was no indoor plumbing; the kids were bathed in a horse trough outside in the summer. There was a big orchard and grapevines. Tibby had fond memories of lying atop the doghouses and eating peaches and grapes. She remembered not so fondly wearing old fashioned dresses made from feed sacks and cast off dresses cut down to fit by her grandmother, Gampy's mother, who lived with them. She was still alive when my sister Pat and I were little kids. She lived in an upstairs bedroom in the near dark because she was blind. Pat and I would creep into her bedroom, staying well clear of her – she pinched – and would rummage around in her closet like little mice. I can still remember the aromatic smell of that closet. By that time, the family had moved to a five-bedroom house in Prospect Park, Pennsylvania. Tib went to high school there but dropped out in the 11th grade to work. She had stories of Id and Dink taking the nice clothes she bought with her earnings and returning them to the floor pitted and dirty. Years later she was still mad about it. It seems she was a bullied and resentful little sister, like a Cinderella with the wicked step sisters. When the war broke out she got a Rosie the Riveter job at a local factory. I have a picture of her at work drinking from the water fountain. Tib was a very attractive young woman with a raft of boyfriends in the service who wrote her letters every day. She told us how Gammy would hold up a packet of letters for her when she got home from work but wouldn't give them to her until she had done her chores. When she was 19 she met my dad, Don Rahner, a sailor serving on Admiral King's flagship as a bosun's mate. After just four months of dating, they married in May. The pictures show a beautiful giddy young couple, Tib in a frothy white wedding gown carrying a huge bunch of roses, Don in his navy blues smiling and handsome. She moved to Washington, D. C. to be near his ship which was a private yacht appropriated for the war and used for top level meetings between heads of state. My dad saw Roosevelt and Churchill on board for one such meeting, I think it was the Yalta Conference. Meanwhile Tib was alone and lonesome in D.C., newly pregnant. She had me in March 1946 just three days after she turned twenty years old. My Dad wanted to stay on in the Navy but Tib wasn't having it so he left and got a blue collar job at the ship yard. He always did hard jobs like riveting and welding but his dream was to own a corner store in his old neighborhood in Philadelphia. We kids overheard arguments between them about this and Tibby won out, it never happened. My parents were poorly matched in many ways. She was the country girl and he was the city boy. Her parents were sober and down to earth, his parents were artistic and alcoholic. My Grandpop Rahner was a musician who played the cello in an orchestra and the organ for the silent movies. Grandmom Mig was the alcoholic who had affairs. Rumor had it that Grandpop was gay, and theirs was a very unhappy marriage. Their house told the story: Miggy's room was frilly and feminine in the sunny front of the house. Pat and I loved her silver-backed hair brushes and perfume bottles and her closet full of fancy dresses. Grandpop's room was at the back of the house, full of books, his cello and a narrow cot covered with a gray blanket. I was 16 when Mig died of pneumonia. She was young, only in her late fifties. My dad was heartbroken. He had to be literally held up by his arms at her funeral. A taxi pulled up at the graveside and a drunken man fell out sobbing and crying. Everyone was muttering and angry. I didn't know what was going on but found out later that he was Mig's lover. This man posted a sentimental remembrance of her in the Philadelphia Inquirer every year for the next 20 years on the anniversary of her death. My mother did not like dad's parents and made no bones about it. After some pretty ruthless battles between Tib and Grandmom Mig, there was very little contact. He loved his mother and kept a close tie with her under the radar. He would tell us with a tear in his eye what a good mom she had been. Hard for us to believe after the thorough brainwashing we had received about the evil Miggy. My dad would take us kids to visit them in the city now and then. Looking back, I think Tib could surely have been more generous. My dad for his part, liked Tib's parents. We lived with them when I was four and five. He loved Gammy's cooking, especially her gravy, and played pinochle with Gampy and my uncles.

My parents divorced after 23 years of marriage and went their separate ways. My mother got a job managing a computer service bureau in New Jersey and never remarried. Within a year or two my dad married a lovely woman named Joan who had five children from a previous marriage. They all called him dad and he finally fulfilled his dream of owning a small corner store in a little town in New Jersey.

They are all gone now, my mom died at 91 and my dad at 74. May they rest in peace.

Sister Pat and me

First Communion with Grandmom Mig, Grandpop Rahner, Gampy and
Gammy Gilpin from left to right, Pat and me in front

Don and Tib on their wedding day 1945

Pat and I watching Gampy's TV circa 1950

Aunt Ginny

Bib (my nickname), Pat and baby Don

Roy and me off to the prom 1964

CHAPTER 3

Senior Prom 1964

All the talk these days is how sad it is that seniors are missing out on those special events like senior prom. It got me thinking of my senior prom all those years ago, long before Covid 19 pandemic lockdowns and social distancing. My senior prom was spectacular, it was Hollywood film-worthy.

I attended a Catholic girls high school in an old gray pile of a building out in the country taught by the Sisters of Notre Dame. No library, no gym, no art, no sports and certainly no social fun. It was a bare bones rigorous classical education. The only exception was the prom which was held in May in the ballroom of one of Philadelphia's best hotels.

My mother took me downtown shopping for a prom dress. It was a pale blue satiny beauty, floor length and modest, of course, with cap sleeves. I got my hair done at the beauty salon, an upswept style for my long hair. I wore elbow length white gloves. My date was Roy, my steady boyfriend that year. He was a Clark Gable lookalike with sensual bedroom eyes and a hairdo like Elvis. We were in love. My parents barely approved but he was a polite and respectful young man despite his appearance. They were afraid we were 'too serious' which was code for having sex – which we were. (This was never discussed, all parties super discreet) A few photos survive of that evening, Roy pinning on my corsage in front of the mantelpiece, he looking handsome in his rented tux.

We left in the shark-finned Bonneville land yacht that Roy had borrowed from his friend Ralph for the evening. My impression of the actual prom was the elegance of the hotel ballroom and dancing the night away doing the twist, the mashed potato, the stroll, the watusi and the pony. We slow danced to "Moon River," Roy holding me tight, his lips close to my ear. After the dancing there was a buffet dinner. Some of my classmates had rented suites to party with their friends and dates but Roy had a better plan. We drove out of the city and headed across the river into Jersey and on to Atlantic City. It was a balmy spring night. We purred along the turnpike with the top down. New Jersey was more rural in those days and the air was fragrant with blooming peach trees once we got past the industrial zone along the Delaware River, a pungent mix of oil refinery and whiskery distillery fumes. The drive down was about an hour and a half. As we got close to Atlantic City, we drove through a marshy area reeking of fish and then - so exciting - we could smell the briny ocean as we neared the shore. Atlantic City is an old resort town and the most urban of all the resort towns along the Jersey Shore. There were no casinos at that time but there was a race track and it had a certain shady reputation as a haven for gamblers and mobsters.

Roy pulled into a side street and parked near the club. I wish I could remember the name; it was a dark cozy luxurious dive of a bar full of men in suits and a few dolled up women. Roy led me to a table in the corner where half a dozen older men sat drinking and smoking cigars. When they saw us coming, we were warmly welcomed with "hey, here comes the kid with his girl !!" Turns out they were friends of Roy's father, 'business associates.' They found seats for us and one man, who seemed to be in charge, a large cheerful, older man of Italian descent called out to the bartender, 'Hey, Guido, bring the kids a couple Manhattans." They all congratulated Roy for his beeyootiful girlfriend. We drank our powerful drinks, the first of its kind I had ever tasted and smoked Kool cigarettes and made conversation with the guys, who were a lot like my dad.

After a few drinks we said thanks, it was time to go. It was really late then, around 4:00 a.m. We strolled down to the boardwalk just a few blocks away and down some steps to the beach, kicked off our shoes and walked in the sand to the surf. The waves were tame so we waded in, Roy rolling up his pants and me holding up my skirt. I wish I could report that we ran into the surf with wild abandon but neither of us wanted to ruin our clothes. (I don't know why I cared about that dress. After the prom it went into a plastic bag in my closet and was never worn again.) So we waded down the surf line holding hands and then found a comfortable spot to lay back and watch the submarine races until the sun came up. Roy was a good kisser and I believe there's no greater time in life for kissing than the teen years.

It was a long, sleepy drive home. We stopped at a diner for breakfast on the way. The other patrons whistled and smiled at us prom goers. The rest of the world was waking up and we could hardly keep our eyes open. Roy dropped me off at home just as everyone in the house was getting up for breakfast. I kissed Roy good-bye and headed up to bed and oblivion.

So what happened to Roy and me and our teen love? I graduated in June and my Aunt Ginnie got me a boring job in the bank where she worked. I saved my money and ran away to Bermuda a year later, never to return. Roy was heartbroken. I hope he's had a good life. He was a good guy.....but I sensed that the world was my oyster .....it was too soon to settle down.

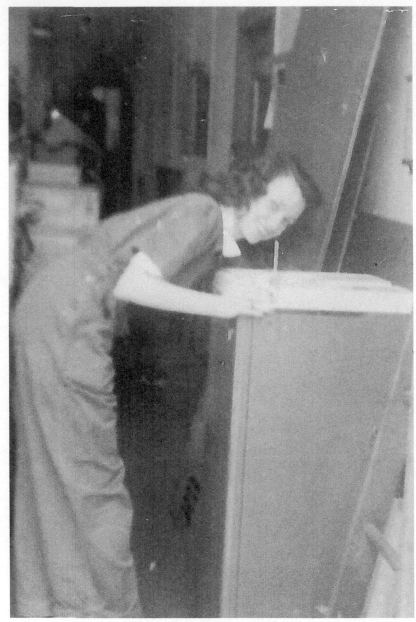

Tibby - aka Rosie the Riveter
circa 1944

CHAPTER 4

Tibby's Triumph

The Act had been drafted by Esther Peterson, head of the Women's Bureau of the Department of Labor. It prohibited employers who were subject to the Fair Labor Standards Act of 1938 (under which the new law fell) from paying employees differently, on the basis of gender, for work that required "equal skill, effort, and responsibility."

I was startled to hear about the passage of the Equal Pay Act of 2018. Wait, wasn't that already passed in 1963? Why again? I flashed back on my teenaged self sitting at the kitchen table as my mom updated my sister Pat and me on her campaign for equal pay at work. Tibby had been working as a keypunch and computer operator since the early fifties at Sun Shipbuilding & Drydock Company in Chester, Pennsylvania. It was a company that had been owned and operated by the Pew brothers since 1916. It became the largest private shipyard and biggest producer of oil tankers in America by World War II. Somehow despite the misogyny and prejudice of that time, she had managed to not only get the job but rise to management level.

My mom was an unusual mother for the times. Very few mothers worked outside the home and she received more than her share of crap for it. Our best friends' mother, a religious woman from the Deep South, wouldn't let us play with them for a time because she felt we were 'neglected' children. We were not. Our dad took good care of us when she went to work at night. He liked to bake cookies and make excellent fudge and play silly games with us like Sock Fight. He too was an unusual father for the times. I was aware of being lucky to have a dad who actually paid attention to us. None of my friends had that.

Every morning Tib came home at breakfast time after working the graveyard shift and told us about some fresh outrage coming from her boss, Wes, who worked the daytime shift. Their shifts overlapped at 8:00 am and he usually dished out a ration of shit before Tib left for home. We hated this man for the misery he visited on our mom. It was an ongoing drama. Working with computers back in the day was not the white collar job it is now. It was heavy physical work, hauling cassettes of punch cards physically into the Remington Rand computer and wiring the "app" to run payroll and reports.

Since my mom ran the payroll reports, she knew how much each employee made and she knew that Wes and the man who ran the second shift earned twice what she did for exactly the same job. In fact, she should have been paid extra for the third shift. This was the cause of simmering resentment for years before passage of the 1963 Equal Pay Act. Tibby didn't delay; she acted immediately by writing a letter to Mr. Pew the president of SunShip laying out the facts. A nailbiting week or two went by before she got the phone call from Mr. Pew himself that he wanted to meet with her in his office after her shift the next day. She said he was very cordial and apologized to her for the injustice she had suffered. He said he was unaware of it until he got her letter and that he was going to raise not only her pay but all the other women in the department to parity with the men. Not only that, he gave her several thousand dollars in back pay as well. She told him she was afraid of reprisal from her boss, Wes. He assured her that would not happen, and it never did.

We were so proud of her !!

So what happened to the Equal Pay Act of 1963? Why a new one in 2018? I searched the internet and found the following excerpt from an article in time.com:

In a sadly-prescient feat of mansplaining in 1964, TIME predicted why the law was unlikely to have the desired effect:

In fact, the new U.S. equal-pay law may cost women some of their jobs because—other things being equal—many companies prefer to hire men. Many women prove reluctant to take on heavy responsibility or to boss men on the job. Supervisors complain that they have a higher absenteeism rate than men—6.5 days a year v. five days—partly because men do not have babies. Some labor leaders are also cool to women workers; only 14% of them join unions, and those who do tend to vote down proposed pension plans. Predictably, they do not want the security of pensions, but the joy of more cash to spend immediately.

TIME was right about the law's impact, if not the cause. When the magazine took stock of the act's legacy in 1974, the wage gap at the time—women earned 60 cents on the dollar—was exactly the same as it was when Kennedy signed the law. "Equal pay for equal work is a familiar slogan of the women's lib movement," the story began. "It has also been the law of the land for large companies for a decade, but a law that was little noted nor long remembered."

The fact was, the law—along with other anti-discrimination laws passed in the intervening years—had not really been put to the test.

In 1974, the Supreme Court decided in Corning Glass Works v. Brennan that the factory in question had broken the law by hiring only men for the higher-paid night shifts, and then women were owed back pay for the money they might have earned in that role. The TIME story cited several other examples of the 1963 law finally creating change: two cases in which AT&T had settled with employees, a steel plant facing a lawsuit, an instance in which Rutgers University was providing back pay to the tune of $375,000.

The pay gap has narrowed since then–women made 78 cents on the dollar as of 2013, according to the White House—but the law's aim, clearly, remains unreached.

I still don't know the reason for the new law, something about closing loopholes, but I wonder how many times this inequity has been settled out of court with a handshake by a fair-minded employer like Mr. Pew and a determined woman like my mother Tibby? These peaceful agreements don't make the news but I know they do happen. She went on to other jobs and had to fight the same battle every time but never so successfully.

She divorced my Dad after 23 years of marriage, moved to New Jersey and finished raising our brother Don. When he was launched as an adult on his own, she sold everything and moved to Bermuda with one suitcase. This was her dream come true. She got a job first as a reservations manager with the Loew's hotel chain then moved on to a computer tech job at the Bank of Bermuda. She enjoyed 20 years in Bermuda before moving back to the States at retirement. She moved to Seattle in 2012 to be near her beloved granddaughter Brenna. Almost immediately she suffered a major stroke and spent the final years of her life in a nursing home. Tibby was 91 years old when she passed away in May 2016.

Tibby and Don engaged 1945

My mom Tibby holding Pat, and my dad Don holding me.

Tibby at 83

First day of school at St. Gabriels in Norwood, PA

CHAPTER 5

Just A Girl Getting An Education

I wrote this essay as an entry in a scholarship contest hosted by Mensa in 2002 ..... I won the $500 cash prize

I have been slowly wending my towards a college degree ever since high school graduation in 1964, a way beset with many detours and roadblocks. My destination, my goal, has always been before me, sometimes seeming as far away as the Hindu Kush, at other times, right at my fingertips. Now as I approach late middle age, the goal is in sight as I enter my senior year as a Humanities major at a local liberal arts college. My journey has led me through three major universities, in as many decades, in pursuit of that elusive degree. The decade of the 90s was devoted to working full time to help my daughter get her degree and begin her working life as a book editor in San Francisco, debt-free. I vowed when she was born that her life would be better, that she would not be deprived of an education as a young person like I was.

It's a shame what happened to me, but it's not an uncommon story for a woman of my generation. Although I ranked in the 98th percentile of all graduating seniors across the country that year, my parents refused

to help me go to college. They felt it was a 'waste of money' to send a girl to college. My brother, who never read a book, was the one chosen to go. The worst part was that my parents knew since my infancy that I had a craving to learn. My mother told me that I would cry for the Sears Roebuck catalog to 'read' in my crib. I begged for books at four and learned to read spontaneously. It just came to me without trying. One of my best childhood memories was the day I got my first library card at seven and carried my stack of books home to devour. My dream was to attend nearby Swarthmore College, that paradise of higher learning. I was so disappointed by my parents' misogyny that I left home at 19 and never returned except for brief holiday visits.

Now, my time has come…and oh my, am I enjoying it. I've scaled back my administrative job to part time (I write minutes for board meetings) and devote my spare time to the study of literature, art history, and philosophy. Sheer bliss! All the reading I've done over the years is being brought together for me formally as part of the 'big picture'. It occurs to me that college is a richer, deeper experience for a reader of my age: the older student brings so much to the experience compared to the younger student who is filled up by it.

Some of my friends ask: why am I working so hard and what will I do with it? I say they just don't get it. I say college is an end in itself. I am savoring every minute. I may consider a teaching certificate after I reach my goal of a BA in Humanities. Last year, I volunteered two evenings a week to tutor Mexican immigrants in speaking English as a second language. I was caught by surprise at how much I enjoyed this work, how happy and fulfilled it made me feel. That was unexpected…and most welcome. A second career may be awaiting me….

This is my story in a nutshell. I never did pursue that second career as an ESL tutor. My remaining two years at the College of Santa Fe were paid for by this prize and an inheritance from my father. Dad had died two years before and sadly, finally came through with the money for college. My brother Don was born when I was ten years old and on the day of his birth, I overheard my father and his brother talking about Don's place reserved at Villanova, my uncle's alma mater. I asked "what about me? I want to go to college" and that's the first time I heard "you're just a girl.....you're going to get married and have kids and it would be a waste of money." I heard this many more times as I grew up and it only made me feel more and more rebellious. My dad's older brother, Uncle Bill, was a Christian Brother who had a doctorate in education and was a guidance counselor at a fancy boys' prep school in Maryland. He tried to persuade my dad, telling him that if I went to college, I would at least have better prospects for finding a breadwinner husband. Great .....And where was my mother? No comment. Both my parents had a high school education but never read books and never read to us at bedtime. But.... we all loved one another and I especially loved my dad who was very sweet and affectionate when we were little. My sister Pat and I would cuddle in bed with Dad, one on each side under his arm and he would tell us stories in a low rumbling ribs voice.

There's an old Japanese saying: 'the nail that sticks up gets hammered flat'.... In first grade, I was the first one to start reading in my class along with a boy named Myron. The nun, Sister Rose Veronica called my mother in and told her I was a reading prodigy. I soon learned the down side of being singled out like this. The nun took Myron and me to the fifth grade classroom to shame the fifth graders with our reading ability. She put words up on the board and I froze looking at the hostile faces of the big kids ... I couldn't perform. I disappointed the nun and shamed myself. I began throwing up in the morning and begging my mother to let me stay home. She dropped me off one morning and outside the car I started crying and begging her to take me home. I looked up and to my total horror saw the nun witnessing this scene from the second floor window. When I walked into the classroom – late – all the kids stared at me and the nun said in a smarmy voice, "Here's Miss Rahner. She didn't want to come to school today." I felt lucky the nun didn't brutalize me in front of the class. I had already witnessed kids being picked up by their ears and bashed against the blackboard. Once she threw a potted plant across the room and smashed it against the wall. I was terrified… I had never seen violence like that before from an adult.

I learned to keep a very low profile after that. Reading became my secret passion. My parents never encouraged me to read, just the opposite. I was a 'book worm' who 'always had her nose in a book'. If my mother saw me reading, she would say, 'what are you doing? Oh, nothing…get in here and help me fold these clothes…' These were the days of free range children and I walked to our local library and got a library card. I read all of the Nancy Drew mysteries, "Little Women", "Black Beauty," "Jane Eyre" and all the horse books by Marguerite Henry among many others. One book that really made an impression on me – I can't remember the title or the author – was the story of a little girl in Bermuda who found a lump of ambergris on the beach and was able to sell it and save her family from financial ruin. Ambergris is valuable whale puke that is used to make perfume. I think I loved this story so much because it was about a girl – just a girl – who did something great. In those dark days of the 1950s, every pronoun was he/him/his never she/ her/ hers or any other. I asked the grownups why this was so and was told that he/him/his was 'the generic.' I didn't really buy that explanation but there it was. Today the world is a very different place, a much better place. Girls and women are everywhere, doing everything under the sun.

Back to the library, my salvation. I moved on to the thrilling Tarzan series by Edgar Rice Burroughs. The librarian told me they were not appropriate for little girls but I checked them out anyway. I would sneak into the adult section and she would chase me out. I was always in a battle to read what I wanted to read. Sister Aquinas in 8th grade asked the class to bring in what we were reading at home so I brought in Jack London's "White Fang". She took it away and returned it a week later, telling me it was 'too adult' for me to read... I read it anyway. For the life of me I couldn't see what was "too adult" about it. My biggest battle was with my mother in high school. I was reading the English 'angry young men' writers like John Braine and Alan Sillitoe. I was reading "Room at the Top" and made the mistake of leaving the book under my bed where my mother found it and tore it up. I was furious, it was a borrowed book. In English class we were reading "Catcher in the Rye," one of my teacher's favorites, unusual for a nun (my high school nuns – the Sisters of Notre Dame – were much better educated than my grade school nuns). At the time there was a lot of controversy about the book and it was banned in several libraries and schools. I knew my mother was aware of the controversy so I left the book under my bed on purpose and sure enough she confiscated it and made a big scene and forbade me to read it. I went to the nun and told her what happened. She told me not to be angry at my mom, her intentions were good, she was 'an innocent' and she wrote a note telling my mom that I had her permission to read the book, that it was a great work of literature, the critics were wrong, and it was required reading for my class. I got my book back and mom left me alone after that. That was as close as I ever got to a mentor or an ally in school. In junior year I was put it in a small honors English class along with half a dozen other girls who were on the academic track. I was on the business track learning typing and shorthand because my parents insisted that I had to be able to earn a living when I graduated, but I also took four years of Latin which I loved, and two years of French. One day, the nun who taught the honors English stuck her head in the door of the business class and saw me typing away. She was visibly angry and asked the teacher what was I doing in that class. They moved out into the hall so I didn't hear the reply. I wish she had called in my parents and encouraged them to support my ambition to go to college, but she didn't.

My last name of Rahner earned me some cachet with the nuns. In homeroom the nun asked me if I was related to the famous Karl Rahner, chief theologian at Vatican II which was going on at that time in Rome. I said he was some sort of cousin and that my Aunt Wilhelmina who still spoke German corresponded with him. Despite the nuns' kindly interest in me, I was still terrified of them, a hangover I suppose from the brutish St. Joseph nuns of St. Gabriel's grade school. Once between classes in the crowd of girls rushing up the stairs, a young nun chased me down and wanted to talk about a book review I wrote on a book about the Holocaust. I was so embarrassed, I ran away from her. I still regret that; I wish I had been a better advocate for myself but I was just a girl, a badly socialized girl.

In senior year all graduating seniors across the country took an all day test on a Saturday on math, history, geography and English, multiple choice and also written essays. When the results came back, I placed in the 98% percentile. I was thrilled that I was in the top two percent of students in the entire USA. My parents' reaction was "that's nice, honey." I began dreaming of and planning my escape.

Within a few weeks of graduation in June 1964, I started work as a secretary, a job my Aunt Ginny got for me at the bank where she worked. This was meant to be my fate. After a few years of work it was assumed that I would marry and have kids and Sunday dinner every week at my folks' house. I didn't argue with my parents about it, that would have been pointless. The next spring our four girlfriends, my sister Pat and I went on vacation to Bermuda. We stayed at the Bermudiana Hotel in Hamilton (since torn down) and met the glamorous French boys who worked in the dining room. They were all graduates of a famous hotel school in Switzerland. We had a wonderful time with them going to the clubs and discos and the beautiful beaches. At the end of the two weeks, we each had our own boyfriend, mine was named Ramon from Nice. These boys, Olivier, Didier, Philippe (Didi and Fifi) and Michel were unlike anything we had ever known. They danced sensuously, they wore amazing colognes and silk scarves they flung around their necks like matadors. They were gorgeous. We all wrote back and forth and swooned over the letters which would end with lines like "a thousand tender kisses.' We were used to the boys back home whose idea of romance was a noogie with a punch on the bicep. We set up another stay later that summer, for a month this time at a cottage the boys rented for us in Paget, named "In A Bit," In Bermuda all the houses have names. We had the best byob parties, raucous parties that had the bobbies (the cops) at the front door telling us to keep it down... there were complaints about the loud music. These same bobbies would show up at the back door later after they 'knocked off' work. We found out that we were being investigated by the CID for possible prostitution which was nonsense, we were just girls having fun.

At the end of the month, we got ready to leave. Ramon was history by then. I had packed a little interview outfit and set out on my moped to find a job. I was hired that same day at the Coral Beach & Tennis Club, a members only resort serving a select clientele, old money, British aristocrats and celebrities. I met Tennessee Williams and Mary Quant (who said I was so pretty I should be a model !!) There was a clubhouse with dining room, bar, lounge and outdoor dining terrace. The guest rooms were cottages tucked in among the lush grounds. The property was atop a cliff overlooking one of best South Shore beaches. Elbow Beach Hotel was at the other end of the long beach of pink sand. My job was front desk reception. I moved into staff quarters that day, a nice roomy cottage next to the tennis courts. My roommate named Liz was a haughty British girl my age who called me The Yank. I found out that the admin staff were all young English girls whose wealthy parents wanted to park them somewhere safe away from home for awhile. There were very few Bermudians on staff probably because the pay was abysmal – 30 pounds a month, about $85, plus room and board. We girls all ate together in the same dining room as the guests at a table in the corner next to the kitchen door. The food was an education for me, French cuisine I had never had before, but always mutton for lunch. My fellow staff members were unfriendly and mocked the way I talked and especially the way I ate eggs. I was feeling persecuted until my new roommate arrived, Roz Jackson from Derbyshire. She was a large bosomy cheerful girl with the most wonderful musical laugh. I found out much later that she was one of the wealthiest girls in England. Her dad owned all the lead mines in Derbyshire. We became good friends and had many fine times out on the town with the lads. Her guy was a Swiss cook named Peter and mine was a handsome Austrian waiter named Heinz. He was tall, blonde and spoke perfect English. We were smitten. He had been a student at the university in Vienna paid for by his uncle who was a communist. He and Heinz argued and the money was cut off so Heinz took off to see the world. He left Bermuda to take a job on Grand Bahama, an island that was in the process of being developed as a resort, a destination dock for giant cruise ships. I followed him soon after. There wasn't much there at the time, one fancy hotel with a casino and a tiny town. The beaches were pristine and piled up with driftwood, shells and wrack. The snorkeling was psychedelic, like nothing I had ever seen before or since. I got a job as cashier at the Villas, an annex to the big Lucayan Beach Hotel. Heinz and I planned our exit with a trip to Vienna to visit his sweet mother and friends. We stayed in Europe six months at his mom's apartment, taking side trips to Italy in the family Volkswagen and hitchhiking to Istanbul through the former Yugoslavia, Greece and Bulgaria. That six months was quite an education for me in every way:

language, architecture, history, culture, gastronomy and friendship with Heinz and his former university friends. We went to a fancy ball Vienna style in the Hofburg Palace with his friends. I bought a beautiful Italian dress with beaded sleeves for the occasion and we waltzed the night away. All these fun and games were a distraction from my goal of getting a college education, but in retrospect, I learned more during that time than I ever would have in a college classroom.

Heinz and I returned to the Bahamas, to the capital Nassau this time and got married. I got a job as cashier and night audit at the Emerald Beach Hotel. I met several black celebrities there like Bill Cosby, Sidney Poitier, Harry Belafonte, Miriam Makeba and Willie Mays. Sidney Poitier stopped by late and asked me what I was doing after work. I had to say I was going home to my husband but I was dead chuffed as the Brits say. Bill Cosby stopped by to chat and even though I was friendly I could see his eyes narrowing looking at me. He walked across the lobby to the head bellman's desk, a black man named Rudy who hated whites. I could hear Cosby say "what's she doing there instead of a sista." The next week I was laid off and replaced with a sista. There was a lot of political turmoil going on at that time with the black PLP party under Lynden Pindling taking over power from the white UBP party for the first time ever and Cosby had some pull. I found out later that the other black celebrities were also there to support the transition. I didn't mind being out of work. Heinz had a good job as captain in the dining room of another luxury hotel so I enjoyed my time off at the beach every day and within a month I was called back. The sista – who was a very nice Bahamian girl my age – hadn't worked out. Neither did our marriage. We didn't last long, less than a year before we split up, a sad story involving a late miscarriage and cheating on both sides. We were too young. The night we broke up I went to a bar with the young man I was cheating on Heinz with and I noticed an older man watching me from the doorway. Another man came to our table and said that his boss Huntington Hartford wanted to know how to meet me and what was my phone number. I gave him my work number and the next day he called to invite me to lunch at his Ocean Club. He said he would send his man to pick me up in his boat to take me to Paradise Island (formerly Hog Island) nearby. He was in the process of developing this little island into what would be a major resort and casino. I said yes but then got cold feet and stood him up. He called the next day furious and demanded to know why. I told him he was too old for me and too rich. So there went my one and only shot at a billionaire ….

I returned to Bermuda. By that time, my aunt Ginny was living there and allowed my sister Pat and me to stay with her for a while. I soon got a job as Girl Friday to a local tycoon who owned several businesses….but that is a tale for another telling….and exactly one year later, in Bermuda, I got a letter from my cousin Chuck who was living in Tucson and attending the University of Arizona. He wrote that I could establish residency there in one year and the tuition would be around $120 a semester. In the meantime I could work and take two classes a semester for credit. Come on down! I packed my bags and was off to Arizona cross-country on a Greyhound bus. The year was 1968 and the counterculture revolution was in full swing. Everyone smoked grass and dropped acid, marched against the Viet Nam war, made love not war and got all shaggy. I did all those things, but the pot - against the popular wisdom of the day - did not make me wooly headed but instead focused me on my education. It was a great study aid. I stopped going out much and stayed home with my books. I got a work/study job on campus in the psychology department that was fascinating. I took the minutes for the ethics committee as well as transcriptions for a professor who was conducting 'encounter groups' with students. I declared my major as psychology. As a freshman, I took all the introductory classes:

anthropology, psychology, biology, German, English composition, and modern literature. I got straight As, got on the dean's list and earned a scholarship that paid my tuition. By the end of my sophomore year, I was getting restless and disillusioned with the psychology department. Psychology was caught up with being considered a hard science so the emphasis was on metrics and a kind of quantifiable objectivity which I found boring and false - BF Skinner psychology. I switched to English as a major. One professor tried to talk me out of it and I was very flattered and touched by the kindly attention but I was done with the psych department.

That spring I found a summer job in Jackson Hole, Wyoming through the campus employment office. I was a hot ticket with my experience as a hotel night auditor. I had the choice of three places that summer: Jackson Hole, Lake Tahoe or Glacier National Park. It was eeny meeny miny mole and I chose Jackson Hole. Little did I know how this would change my life. Another tale for another time. I didn't go back to Tucson in the fall. I loved Jackson Hole so much that I ended up staying there almost two years. I learned to ski a little, made some good friends and with the help of guidebooks, I learned about all the plants and their uses that I encountered on my daily hikes in the woods. People began asking me to teach them what I knew. I lost my scholarship but gained an adorable little baby girl we named Avesa from a wintertime romance with a young man from Minnesota. Before she was born I slid down to Tucson to be with family and friends and snuck in two more classes at the U of A: basic design and philosophy, both enjoyable, especially the art class, something I had never experienced before, there was no art or music in my Catholic school education. I returned to Minneapolis to be near Avesa's father Marv for the birth and while there I took classes at the University of Minnesota, including astronomy, Native American studies, a history of journalism course, and Greek/

Roman mythology. The astronomy class unbeknownst to me was taught by a famous professor who was retiring that year and it was tough. I was taking an astrology class on the side and wanted to learn about the constellations, the sort of thing I would have learned at summer camp if I had ever gone. Instead we learned about gas spectrometry and mass chromatography, actually pretty interesting but I had to work hard for a C. At the last class everyone stood up and applauded the professor. The Native American studies class was taught by a young Ojibwe woman who gave me a B when I had in fact earned an A going by the points. When I complained, she said 'so now you know how it feels' which I thought was unfair. Being just a girl, I've known all my life 'how it feels'. As a young mother with temp secretarial jobs and a baby I didn't have time to get involved with student life at UM. It was a first for me, a large impersonal urban school but I did gain another 14 credits toward my goal of earning a degree.

My next stop on the road to a college degree was the University of New Mexico. I had met a young man named Dave Rockwell in Minneapolis who wanted to get out of Minnesota. So did I. We packed up and moved to Tucson – again - where I had family and friends. Long story short, we got married and are still married 45 years later.

Dave's company moved him to Albuquerque and I enrolled at UNM in pursuit of that elusive degree. I decided it was time to get serious and aim for a business/accounting degree. I took economics, college algebra, calculus, statistics, computing for business students, marketing, and financial accounting. Just for fun I took American Humor. I enjoyed every class immensely but had to withdraw when the demands of home became too much. I remember hearing Avesa and Dave laughing at some TV show while I was studying in the back bedroom and wishing I could join them. Avesa, who was six at the time, would come back and tap on the door asking if she could come in, promising to be very quiet.

I realized I was missing out on being with her, six never comes again, so I called it quits for the time being when the semester was over.

Fast forward to 2001. Avesa is grown up, a college graduate living in San Francisco. I enrolled at the College of Santa Fe in their evening program. I was working as administrator at Sandia Laboratory Federal Credit Union writing minutes for five boards and several committees. I don't think there's any better way to improve your writing skills than writing long form narrative minutes. I gave up the idea of advancing my career with a college degree and took classes for the pure enjoyment of learning. At CSF I studied literature, art history, philosophy, the ancient world, logic and speech. The classes were rigorous and each class required a lot of writing including some long term papers at which I excelled, thanks to my day job.

I graduated in the spring of 2003 at the age of 57 with a BA cum honore in Humanities. Phew, finally, I did it ! My mom and daughter Avesa flew in for the ceremony and they hosted a great party for me afterwards inviting everyone we knew.

I went on to write and publish a book in 2005 titled "Boiling Frogs – Intel vs. the Village" available on amazon......but that's another story.

Mother Superior of St. Gabriels

First Communion with Mom, Dad and sister Pat

First Communion 1953: from left to right: Grandmom Mig, Mom, Dad, and Gammy. Pat and me in front

Heinz and me visiting the folks, bratty
little brother Don in lower left

The beach at Coral Beach Club, Bermuda

The first book I've published "Boiling Frogs - Intel vs. the Village"

Fingers and me in Corrales

CHAPTER 6

Horses

What is it with girls and horses? Someone once said "There's something about the outside of a horse that's good for the inside of a girl." Actually, it was Churchill who said this and he said "the inside of a man" but truth be told, more girls are attracted to horses than boys. Equestrian sports are the only Olympic sports where women and men compete on an equal footing. My two granddaughters Esme 13 and Silvi 10 are now in the throes of big horse love. My own love affair with the equines began when I was about five lying on the smelly rug in my grandmother's house with my sister Pat on a rainy Pennsylvania afternoon watching the Lone Ranger on TV gallop across the sun drenched Southwestern landscape. We were inspired to make our own horsies out of stuffed socks mounted on broom handles. We gave them curly manes and long eye lashes, flaring nostrils and bridles and reins modeled on the Lone Ranger's. We galloped all around the fields and woods, now and then pulling up our steaming steeds to have a look around before dashing off in search of the lost dogie. Later on in grade school we knocked on neighbors' doors and asked to clean their hedges for fifty cents each. We lived on a busy road and those were the days when people tossed their trash out the car window and it ended up snagged in the hedges. For four hedges cleaned each, we could go horseback riding in nearby Secane in a ring for an hour. Our dad drove us to the stable and encouraged our old and tired horses to keep moving. He did it very sweetly "c'mon girl" and I was so embarrassed by him and frustrated that I couldn't make my horse go as briskly as I wanted. A few years later we moved on to a new stable farther out in the country with better horses and trails to ride on. I met a boy named Jim when I was 16 who worked at a training stable for race horses. I started working there too for no pay other than the privilege of riding the big pony after all the stalls were mucked out. After a while I was allowed to groom the easier horses. By 'easier' I mean colts that were not too fiery, crazy and dangerous. Some of them were downright scary, too much for me. They were sent off to the race track when they were two to three years old and many didn't make it. I realized what a brutal sport horseracing is. Very few made the cut. They either broke down and had to be destroyed or they came back to the stable with PTSD – crazy behavior like cribbing and weaving and striking out with their teeth and hooves. It was very sad. The stable also had standardbred horses that were being trained for harness racing. They were a different horse entirely with calm and sweet dispositions. It was thrilling to watch them race around the training track with their driver in his sulky going really fast and never breaking from a trot.

I got interested in the racing industry and immersed myself in reading all the magazines and learning all the thoroughbred bloodlines and who was winning what at the track. One weekend, my boyfriend Roy and I and an old friend of his who had spent his life on the track went to the Bowie racetrack in Maryland ....the only time I've been to a racetrack, before or since. I studied the tip sheet for the day and there was a horse whose breeding was pure Kentucky royalty. This was his first or second race and I just knew he would win. He was a 13 to 1 shot. I put down my $5 bet and he came in first….I won $65 – a lot of money in those days, a week's salary. We went out to dinner and dancing that night to celebrate. That day spelled the end of my horse days for a long while. That same year, I graduated from high school, took a boring job in a bank, saved my money and ran away to Bermuda. I was launched…..

In 1968 I landed back in Bermuda and found a job as Girl Friday to a local tycoon who among many things had a stable of about a dozen horses. He owned carriages for tourists and weddings. He also owned a dairy farm of 400 cows, a fleet of 50 taxis and the Island Water Company. He went by the initials MRT and was quite the showman. He had a big Palomino stallion that he would saddle up with a massive western saddle worked with silver to ride into town to make the bank deposit.

I negotiated part of my salary to have the use of one of his riding horses. This was heaven. After work most every day my friend Betty Lou would meet me for a ride until sunset. My favorite horse was a Palomino mare whose name I can't remember now. We went all over the east end of the Island exploring the many trails and roads. We had to skirt the edges of the Mid Ocean Golf Club and we longed to gallop across the big green which would have gotten us into a lot of trouble. I remember going back along a country road at dusk and passing a small wooden chapel full of people singing a beautiful gospel song. Lots of good memories like that….Bermuda magic.

I joined the Bermuda Horse & Pony Club and took jumping lessons at the Warwick Riding Academy. The Club put on midnight rides when the moon was full that took in the South Shore beaches. I had an admirer named Teddy who let me ride his best horse on the ride, a nice Tennessee Walker. They were a popular breed in Bermuda for their smooth, flowing gait. It was so thrilling to canter on the water's edge, the horses all excited. The Bermudians said they had 'bees in their head' from the full moon. The ride ended with a 'booze up' under the trees at a big house in Southampton and then the long, long ride home in the wee hours. Some people had to be helped onto their horses after one too many Dark n' Stormy. The horses knew the way home so no mishaps occurred, just the clopping of tired hooves. the musical din of a million tree frogs and the scent of jasmine in the air.

The Club also put on scavenger hunts on weekend afternoons in the winter and spring. We went in pairs on horseback and worked off a list of eccentric items like a pawpaw fruit, a crab leg, a rusty horseshoe nail, a loquat, etc.. We all met up at the end of the afternoon at the Riding Academy, prizes were awarded and of course, a booze up. Teddy asked me to marry him that day but I said no. All we had between us was the horses. He thought that was enough, but I didn't. He had a barn in Spanish Point and I used to ride his other horse who was an old stiff thoroughbred retired from the track. Bermuda had a horse racing track for many years next to Shelly Bay before it was closed down in 1961. All the race horses who survived were scattered around the Island as riding horses. I would meet up with two young Bermudian friends named Pam and Paul and ride all around the lush green hills of Government House grounds not far from Spanish Point.

After a year or two of all this fun, I got rock fever and left the Island for Tucson, Arizona and college at the University of Arizona. I always wanted to go to college and this was my opportunity. My cousin Chuck and his family lived there. He wrote me that I could go to school for only a few hundred dollars a semester so that's what I did for the next few years. I met an English woman who had a stable outside the city and I started riding with her and her young sons. She asked me to ride one of her horses in a jumping class in a show. Unfortunately, I was too nervous to do well, made some bad mistakes on the course and that was the end of my showing career. But I didn't really care, I was sorry to let the lady down but it was great to get out in the desert to ride, that's what I really liked.

After two years of school in Tucson, I got a job through the campus employment agency as a night auditor at a resort hotel in Jackson Hole, Wyoming. I had been surviving on a work/study program job but needed something for the summer. Because of my experience as night auditor in the Bahamas, I got three offers: one from Lake Tahoe, another from Glacier National Park and the Jackson Hole offer. It was a tough decision, all three were so tempting, but I chose the Alpenhof in Teton Village and that turned out to be the fork in the road for me that set me on a course that changed my life. I met Linda who was secretary at the hotel and she took me home with her to the village of Wilson one day after work to meet her friends. I knew I had found "my people" as soon as I walked through the door of her log cabin. "Sweet Baby James" was on the turntable, sweet herbal smoke in the air and delicious duck for dinner, shot by the guys that day on Fish Creek. Three of us, Jane, Steve and I agreed to rent the large cabin up the road from Linda's. They were recent graduates of colleges back east. This was the 'summer of love' and we had a stream of freaks aka hippies coming through all summer, camping on the lawn and sleeping on every flat surface in the place. BTW, "freak" is not a pejorative; it's what hippies called themselves. I would come home from work at 9 am after breakfast at the hotel (night auditors work midnight to 8:00 am) and have to evict some stranger from my bed so I could sleep. I was the only one with an actual job! I met a local cowboy named Bob who offered to lease me a horse for the summer to which I eagerly agreed. The cabin we rented was surrounded by a few acres of grass for the horse to graze. I scraped together some tack and we were off exploring the area. I soon discovered there was very little riding because all the nearby land was private and fenced. That left us with only the shoulders of roads to ride on. Fish Creek Road was one of those few roads and it was terrifying when a huge log truck came barreling down the road at us. If you had a truck and trailer, there was a lot of riding in the Park but I was so poor, I had to hitchhike back and forth from Wilson to the Village to work every day. Halfway through my paid up lease, Cowboy Bob started 'borrowing' the horse to take to the rodeo on Friday nights in Jackson. Then he replaced that pretty nice horse with a half broke nag that was no fun to ride. Bob came over one morning and somehow the horse got out. We both jumped in his truck and took off after the galloping horse down Fish Creek Road. At one point, the horse hesitated, Cowboy Bob leaped out of his truck with his lasso swinging. The horse accelerated across the creek and tore off across a field and was never seen again. He blamed me for the loss, wanted me to pay him $400, I refused and our contractual relationship ended on a sour note as you may imagine. That was the end of riding for the next six years.

In 1977, Dave Rockwell and I got married and began our 43 year – and counting -journey together. My five-year old daughter Avesa became our daughter. We moved to Albuquerque for Dave's job, bought an acre of land in Corrales and began planning the construction of our adobe home. Corrales is a horsey community, lots of riding along the ditch banks and in the bosque, a cottonwood forest along the Rio Grande. With the boundless energy of my youth, I dug postholes for the corral and together Dave and I put up the fence and a shelter in one corner. I went shopping for a horse and bought a chestnut gelding named Quero. He was a decent starter horse but I made the mistake of feeding him too much sweet feed and vitamins and he turned into a bucking dynamo. I was flung into the dirt more than once. The barn where I was taking lessons helped me with advice on my horsekeeping…I didn't know that horses are like engines and when you feed them high octane fuel… look out. I changed his feed to grass hay and he settled down. We had some good times. I made a padded seat that attached to the back of my saddle and I would pick up Avesa at Corrales Elementary to give her a ride home. Then Quero began to go lame with a slipped stifle so I gave him to the barn on consignment and he was sold to a little girl as her first horse. I began my search for a good horse. I had a few thousand dollars to spend, enough I thought to buy a keeper. I had read somewhere that there is no greater pleasure than owning a fine horse and that's what I was after. On a tip I drove down to Socorro to look at a thoroughbred mare that was for sale. The owner was a woman named Anne from back east who had brought the mare down from Canada. Fingers was very well bred. Her grandsire All Hands won the Belmont and her great grandsire Mahmoud won the Epsom Derby. She sold at the Keeneland auction in Kentucky as a yearling and was put on the track for a brief time. She was bought in a claiming race by a Greek gentleman and sent to Canada as a hunter/jumper prospect. Anne showed me her registration in the Canadian Hunter Improvement Society so she was destined to be a brood mare. She had had a colt the year before I bought her and I soon could see she was grieving for her baby. She wanted to be a mama ! For the first few years when she was in season, she would stop on the trail and spread her hind legs, flipping her tail over her back, calling out loudly to any potential nearby stallions. Embarrassing. If she heard a colt or filly calling out, she would get very emotional. Maybe she imagined it was her lost colt. She was a tall beautiful dark bay with a small star between her kind eyes. In retrospect she was a bad choice for a horse that was going to do nothing more than trail rides in the bosque, like buying a Ferrari for grocery runs, but I was smitten and I bought her that day. Anne delivered her the next week and we signed off on the paperwork. I saw that Fingers and I had the same birthday, March 26. Anne said it was meant to be.... I don't believe in that sort of thing but it was a startling coincidence. We started out slowly on the trails, lots of trotting and some slow cantering. I wasn't sure how much horse I had on my hands and I didn't want to get into a wild runaway situation. She was a lot of horse, but she turned out to be pretty level headed, a little spooky and a little hot but not bad. She tended to pull a lot which was understandable given her time on the track. I used a soft snaffle and did a lot of half halts to bring her back under control. I tried a twisted snaffle for better control but she wasn't having it, she was furious and threw a fit. I went to a snaffle with three copper 'keys' in the middle for her tongue to play with and she was very happy with that. She was a horse who commanded respect. There were times when I came out with my saddle to ride on a chilly morning and there she was cantering in a tight circle, snorting and tossing her head. That's when I got out the longe line and trotted her in a circle until she dropped her head and I knew she was ready to ride without a rodeo. They say you should have a horse who's a challenge without being a threat and that was Fingers. I never hit her or yelled at her and she responded with real affection. When I put on her bridle and put the bit in her mouth, she would rest her head on my shoulder and nuzzle my cheek. I became aware that she was lonesome all on her own in a pen on the windswept mesa. I'm sure she had always been kept in big barns with lots of other horses around. One morning, she was gone. She had busted out and I had no idea where she was. We went searching and found her a mile away grazing with a group of other horses. I knew I had to get her a companion. We tried a goat but could not contain it in the pen. I didn't know that goats can crawl under fences – they can- and he ended up smashing one of the glass panels in our greenhouse to get in the house to be with us. The goat went back and I ended up buying an old burro named Chapita who bonded nicely with Fingers. I knew very little about her history except that she was a kind of horse nanny and had had several owners before us. She was very old and almost blind. Every spring we would pull chunks of grey hair off her and toss them on the ground. Birds would take every last bit of it for their nests. One day I did an experiment – an IQ test - with Chapita and Fingers. Their absolute favorite food was the green leaves from peeling fresh corn so I put a bunch in a large brown paper shopping bag and crunched the top shut. They were standing peaceably side by side in the shade when the bag was tossed in. Fingers, being the alpha, ran out, grabbed the bag in her teeth and shook it and shook it to no avail. She gave up after a while. Chapita then walked out, put one hoof on the edge of the bag, grabbed the other edge with her teeth and tore it open. Fingers squealed in rage, ran out, took it away from her, then spun around and kicked poor Chapeets soundly in the side. I was afraid that she had broken her ribs, but Chapita was okay, the only damage apparently was to Fingers' ego. They shared the corn shuck peaceably. It was all about food with Chapita. Once she got out and would not let me catch her. I got a pan of oats and approached her shaking it. She followed me all the way back to the corral and I gave it to her. If I hadn't given it to her, I'm sure that trick would never have worked again.

On one of our rides, I met Barbara Pijoan out on her old thoroughbred gelding Hustler. She lived nearby and we became riding companions and friends for the next ten years. She was much older than me, my mother's age it turned out, and from a wealthy family back east. Her father was one of the founders of IBM. She had met Michael her husband- to- be on a summer program from Bennington to the Navajo rez where he was an Indian Health Service doctor. She was eighteen and he was on his fourth marriage. That and many other stories were shared as we explored every inch of Corrales on those horses. Then one day, we struck off at a canter, she was behind and I heard a loud 'oof'....Barbara had fallen off and was flat on her back. I tried to help her sit up and she could not, almost fainting. I rode to a nearby house and shouted for help. The medics came and took her to the hospital where she remained for a month with a pelvis broken in several places. She didn't ride again for a long time. In the meantime, husband Dave said he would like to ride with me... We bought an Aussie saddle which is perfect for a new rider since it's almost impossible to come off it. We started looking for a horse and found a pretty little Arab mare named Fanta in Corrales. She had been neglected and truly I felt we were saving her life. On a hot day, she had no water or shade in her corral. She and Fingers became best buds. Fingers was content now that she had her herd: Chapita and Fanta. She and Fanta liked to compete trotting on the ditch banks and Fanta was the hands down winner in that arena. She could fly ! Fingers was a much larger horse but she could not out trot Fanta. Dave and I had a lot of fun riding together. He was fearless for a brand new rider, sometimes too fearless. Once we were on the clear ditch trail and Dave wanted to take off at a lope. I told him not a good idea, there were lots of gopher holes on that stretch but he took off despite my warning. Next thing I saw Fanta going head over heels and Dave tumbling down the steep bank. Everyone was okay, incredibly, just a torn T shirt. Another time he rode into a box canyon and at the end instead of turning around, he started up a faint steep trail to the top and we had no choice but to follow. At the top, the horses had to scramble, their bellies scraping the edge to get on top of the mesa. When we finally stopped to catch our breath, Fingers shook herself all over like a wet dog and looked around at me incensed, like "what the hell, lady!" It was comical, but it made me realize we were a team and I had let down my side. She was a brave horse. There was a dog, a Doberman, we passed every day outside a rundown trailer on the ditch. He went after us every time and we managed to finesse the attack every time until one day Fingers simply ran him over- with my encouragement. He tumbled under her hooves yipping and howling. His owner, an old Hispanic guy, came out and said "you get him lady, you get him !" The dog never came after us again. We would ride by and he would lie there not moving a muscle, just lifting an eyelid as we went by. Another time, two St. Bernards came after us. I'm sure these dogs, who lived in a new suburban looking house, had never seen a horse before. They jumped all over Fingers like she was another dog and when one jumped up on her chest she lifted her front hoof and brought it down on the top of his head, knocking the dog out cold. The owner came out of his garage irate demanding to know what we did to his dog. I told him that's what happens when you let your dogs run loose, mister. Fingers literally pranced away shaking her head from side to side, she was so proud of herself. I was proud of her too.

In 1988 I went to work full time and could only ride on the weekends. I thought this would be the ideal time to breed Fingers and fulfill her dream of being a mama. We had become acquainted with an old cowboy named George Miller who had a training stable nearby. He was an expert horseman and took in problem horses to straighten them out for their owners. He used a trail that went by the back of our property and we would visit with him as he rode by on his explosive charges. He would drawl, "Ain't nothing wrong with this horse, he just lacks employment." And if we remarked on their bad behavior, he'd say "no problem, this horse is so trussed up, all he can do is fart." I came across a western magazine with George on the cover and the headline "Meet the Man who Started Skipper W" a famous Palomino roping stallion. I love Palominos. I asked George about him and he remarked that a son of Skipper W was standing stud down in Los Lunas and his offspring were all Palomino. One thing led to another and pretty soon Fingers was on her way for a week long date with the stallion. I wasn't there to witness it but it seems Fingers was too tall for them to mate the usual way. They dug a little ditch and backed her up to him but that didn't work either, so they just turned them out together in a field and let nature take its course. Risky business since mares can kick the hell out of a stallion and do some real damage. But apparently the two had a big love affair and Fingers was in the mood. She came home with shiny half dollar sized hickies all over her neck, all calm and happy. The vet came and pronounced her pregnant. Then as so often happens, Fingers slipped the embryo - and it was not to be. I found out this is really common. You don't see anything, the mare actually absorbs the tiny fetus. We didn't try again. but after that, Fingers didn't scream and flip her tail anymore when she was in heat. She had had the romance of her life and she seemed to be satisfied after that.

We had a dozen good years before disaster struck in the form of Intel Corporation. They built the largest semi conductor manufacturing plant in the WORLD right above us on the mesa top where Barbara and I used to have a good gallop on a long straight sandy road. Intel said it was a clean industry but we found out pretty quick that was a half truth, it was only clean for the chip. For those living below the plant it was a stinky toxic mess. I got involved with a local group trying to salvage our fresh, clean air but to no avail.....a long story that ended with my writing a book about it "Boiling Frogs" years later. In the meantime, we were all getting sick with headaches, rashes and coughs. Poor Fingers was no exception. She began to get all wheezy with lots of discharge from her nose that the vet called the snots. He gave me pills to grind up and put in her feed. I made her a hot mash with applesauce and molasses every day to get her to eat the bitter pills. In 1996 we realized we had to move away and sold our beautiful home that we had put almost 20 years of hard work into. I couldn't take Fingers to our new place in Placitas so I planned to give her away to a friend who promised to give her a good home. By this time, Chapita had died of old age. We gave Fanta to the people who bought our house. They had two young kids who wanted to learn to ride.

I was at work when Dave called to say that Fingers was on the ground and couldn't get up. I raced home, called the vet who showed up quickly. He walked around her slowly and then picked up a hind leg which was loose and flopping, broken. It had rained heavily the night before and she had run out into the muddy corral and slipped. She had to be put down. It was close to evening by then. He gave her two shots, one to tranquilize and the second to finish her off. She died with her head in my lap, very quietly and calmly. She was 25 years old, the lifespan of a thoroughbred but nonetheless, I curse Intel for the weakness that led to her death. She didn't show any signs of old age and could have had another five years or more of a good life. I spent most of the night outside, sitting next to her and talking to her. In the morning, I called the knacker to come take her body away and I left for work. I didn't want to be there to see it. Dave took Fanta around to the front of the house when he came so she wouldn't see it either. The knacker puts a chain around the back hooves and pulls the body across the ground and up into the back of the truck with a motorized winch....it's very violent and awful to witness. Fanta was frantic for several days afterwards, running along the fence and calling out for her lost friend and companion.

That was truly the end of my riding days. I'm too old now. I held on to my good German-made saddle for a long time and finally sold it for $700, the same amount that I had paid for it twenty years before. This summer I gave away the last bits of my riding gear: Esme got the longe line and Silvi got the two good grooming brushes. I gave them my well- read copy of Marguerite Henry's wonderful book "An Album of Horses." I hope they enjoy it as much as I did as a young rider, dreaming of horses.

Fingers and me

Fanta, a lovely Arab mare

Chapita the burro and Dave's horse Fanta

Dave building the horse barn.

Barb and her horses.

CHAPTER 7

Rosemary

The recent police murder of a schizophrenic black man on the street got me thinking about Rosemary and how I used to worry that would happen to her. The police are not equipped to deal with psychotic people acting out and often - too often - resort to deadly force. There's some hope in the air lately with calls to "defund the police" which is an unfortunate phrase when what is meant is to fund social workers who can assist the police with the crazies.

My connection with Rosemary Branagan began in the early 90s when I was working as admin for Sandia Laboratory Federal Credit Union. The Chairman of the Board asked my boss Chris the CEO to look after the banking for his sister-in-law Rosemary. She'd been banned from the lobby for allegedly spitting on a child and banned from his own house for some unspecified offense. She was not allowed back in the family fold unless she took her meds, which she refused to do. Chris agreed to help and every Thursday at exactly 3:00 p.m. she would sweep into the office dressed in her signature filthy raincoat with a girlish ribbon in her long white hair and a funky aroma in her wake. Not bad but definitely uniquely funky. She was a large, tall gregarious woman in her sixties of Irish descent who liked nothing better than an evening at the piano belting out a tune or two - as she later told me. She flirted outrageously with the suits in the office, getting in close and stroking their ties. She was warm and personable to those she liked but she was, no doubt, batshit crazy with the 'voices'. I could never have imagined then what benefactors we would become for one another during our ten years of friendship ending in her death in 2003.

My boss would emerge from his office and take her deposit downstairs to the tellers. On his return they would chat for another half hour or so and then she would leave. She never talked to me or the other two girls in the office. Chris told me she had a trust from her parents and was quite well off despite her appearance. She lived in a crummy motel in downtown Albuquerque named The Gaslite (no kidding). She drove a battered old car that she abandoned after a few years. She said it was infested with a demon…after that she took two buses to get to the credit union. This went on for a year or so until one Thursday she took notice of me and for some reason decided I was okay. From then on, I was the one who did her banking and visited with her every Thursday at 3:00 p.m.- much to my boss' relief. Our relationship grew from there. Every week I did her banking, which always included $200 in twenties and once a month her social security check and a pension check from New York City Hospital where she worked many years as a registered nurse. Then we would settle in for a look at her 'mail bag'. She carried on a vast correspondence with old friends, writers, celebrities, royalty and her special favorites, pedophile priests whom she thought were all wrongly accused. Her thing was birthday cards that she signed with a large copperplate flourish "Rosemary." She got thank you notes back from famous actors, politicians and even the Queen of England. The Queen's thank you note came from a lady- in- waiting who wrote "Her

Majesty commands me to send her acknowledgment of your recent good wishes on the occasion of her birthday." The best one ever was from Moammar Khadafy the despotic ruler of Libya. He must have been a lonely tyrant. Rosemary sailed in holding aloft a large fat manila envelope, singing out "look what I got from Moammar!" Everyone in the office fled. This was during the time of the terrorist anthrax mailings to officials in Washington D.C. and the public was paranoid. For some reason, I thought it would be fine and it was. He sent a signed headshot of himself and many brochures on the glories of life in Libya. Rosemary had done a lot of traveling in her early years pre-schizophrenia and she was familiar with that part of the world. She had traveled in Egypt, seen the pyramids and the Nile, rode a camel. She told me all about her apartment in Manhattan and her baby grand piano where her friends gathered to sing. I found out that this baby grand was in the Mayflower storage facility along with all her other furniture and belongings. She wrote them a check every month for $400 for ten years and never claimed her stuff. I told her I would help her find a nice apartment where she could have her things around her but she was adamantly against it so I gave up trying after a while. She felt at home at the motel and was friends with the owners who were Pakistanis. She knew their families and sent cards and gifts to the children on their birthdays. In the late 90s, the mayor of Albuquerque had the Gaslite torn down and the owners found her a new motel farther east on Central, just as crummy. Her sense of stability was terribly shaken by this move. Another shock to her system was being thrown out of the Catholic cathedral downtown where she had attended mass every Sunday. I wrote the pastor a shame on you letter asking why we, a secular institution were able to go the extra mile to fulfill her needs and you, the Church would not, and were denying her, a devout Catholic, the sacraments, your basic duty. He wrote back "enough is enough" that she had spit on other congregants and he would not allow her back. I didn't tell her about this exchange. She told me about being evicted from all her favorite restaurants along Central. I started bringing her lunch from home that we would eat in the break room. She showed me her sandals that she wore year round even in the snow were falling apart and I ordered new ones online. She said her nightgown had ripped apart so I bought her a new one at Target. Someone had left a good Burberry raincoat at the credit union which I claimed for her from the lost and found. I offered to get her old one cleaned but she refused although she was very happy to wear the new one. I felt very sorry for her and I liked her, she had no one in the world on her side but me. She talked and talked and I listened. She was not at all curious about my life and that was fine with me. She said to me many times "I love you honey." I was touched by that. I challenged her delusions only once. She told me the voices told her that the Pope had landed at the airport in Albuquerque and was staying in the room behind her at the motel. I said "you don't believe that's really true, do you? She looked so hurt and confused I decided not to go there again. I had no idea what was going on in her head. I helped her all that I could, but I had my limits, for instance I didn't invite her to my house for Thanksgiving. I felt bad about that but she was just too unpredictable. We were okay one on one but not in a group. I found this out when I took her on an outing to the zoo. She was alone in her motel room every day and I thought a trip to the zoo would be a nice break. We went on a weekday when I thought there would be fewer people but there were lots of young mothers with kids in strollers. They seemed to really agitate Rosemary. She noticed an older man looking at her and she said 'what are you looking at? Wanna a piece of this?' as she swept her hand down her side in an enticing motion. That was funny....but I was running interference all afternoon and I was afraid she would do something really inappropriate. Later she told me about a baby she'd had when she was in the Navy in San Diego with a fellow corpsman who was a medic along with her. Her parents forced her to give the baby away at birth (don't you just love those prolife Catholics). She only saw him once but named him Ritchie. She got all emotional telling me the story and it seemed to have been a breaking point for her. I wondered if that was the beginning of her slide ....I never did much reading or research on schizophrenia. I preferred to see Rosemary as a unique, vibrant and interesting person. I had no interest in labeling her by her disorder or disease. She told me once about an incident in her late teens when she had a major seizure that rendered her unconscious for several hours and how upset her mother was …. That may have been the beginning…

The trouble at the credit union began when we moved from our old building into a new wing. In the old building there was a straight path between the front door and the admin office. In our new addition Rosemary had to negotiate a long hallway with several busy offices along the way. Before long, the head of the Human Resources called my boss to say that Rosemary was creating a 'hostile work environment' by frightening tender young employees along the way to the admin office. We were called in for a discussion by the head of HR, a dragon of a woman. My boss - who luckily outranked her - came to Rosemary's defense. He had a kind heart, I'll say that for him. and we were able to strike a compromise. I agreed to meet her at the elevator and escort her to the admin office. This worked well for a while until the day Rosemary went to the ladies room unescorted. I should have gone with her. Apparently she peered through the crack in the toilet stall door and said teasingly "I can see you." The employee freaked out and called her supervisor on her cell phone from the stall to come rescue her. She was almost hysterical and had to be helped to her car for the rest of the day off. HR was alerted and the truce was off. The next Thursday, my boss called Rosemary into his office and told her she could no longer come to the credit union to do her banking. He would allow her to keep her accounts but I would do her banking for her and drive to her motel with the receipt and cash. I agreed to do this. She was very angry and on the way out of the building she shoved a man in the doorway. The member complained and when my boss heard about this he closed her accounts. She was out. He made one concession: I could continue to visit her at her motel during working hours on Thursday and be paid for my time. I went to visit her the next Thursday to talk about getting a new checking and savings account at a bank near her motel. Rosemary was scrupulous about her finances. She knew exactly how much she had on deposit and she paid her bills on time. For the past year she had been communicating with a lawyer back in New Jersey about a bequest that an old friend had left her. When she brought documents in, I would witness and notarize them for her. Finally the check came in from her old friend Kay Blizzard of Dennisville, New Jersey, the next town over from my Dad's town of Franklinville. Kay never married; she was a member of Rosemary's girlfriend posse in Manhattan. Rosemary told me stories of all the fun they had going out on the town and taking trips and cruises. Kay inherited from her parents and divided her estate between the five girlfriends. Rosemary's share was $40,000. Now she had a check in her hand and nowhere to deposit it. I suggested we go to the bank behind her motel and she agreed.

All went well at the bank until the customer rep asked Rosemary for ID. All she had was an expired driver's license. Since she had given away her car, she did not renew her license. The rep said she would need to get valid ID before she could open an account. We argued that the expired license should be good enough since it clearly identified Rosemary with a picture and I would vouch for her. No dice, said the customer rep and Rosemary stormed out, shoving a man in the doorway on her way out. Now, not only would she not get an account, they wouldn't let her back in the building. Back at my office, I asked the VP to intercede. He made a phone call and came back to say sorry, they didn't want her as a customer. I asked Rosemary if she would be willing to go to the MVD office with me to get an ID and go to another bank. She said absolutely not. I told her she had to have a bank or credit union to do her banking, what else could she do?. We talked it over. I offered one solution: open an account in my name at the credit union with her as co-signer. She agreed, she trusted me so that's what we did, and it worked well until her death a year later....

It was a hot afternoon. I arrived at Rosemary's motel to do her banking, bringing lemonade and cold cucumber soup. A low-rider slowly rolled by saying "hey, are you here to see that old lady lived in that room? She died....." I went to the motel office and the Pakistani manager told me the shocking news. They had found her face down on the bathroom floor, dead. She was 74 years old. She had been complaining to me recently of not being well but of course, she would not see a doctor. I offered to take her, but in the ten years I had known her she never went to a dentist or a doctor....she didn't trust them. The manager said her sister had been notified and would be there the next day to clear out her room. He said I should get in there first and get all the money she had hidden away throughout the room. I was surprised he knew about that. I always wondered what she did with all the twenties she got every week. I said no, that's for her sister to do.... and I thought it was awfully decent the motel people hadn't plundered her room. Rosemary was a fan of Kazantzakis and we had talked about the scene in Zorba the Greek where the widow dies and the village people some in like a pack of hyenas to strip her room.

Rosemary's sister Maureen called me the next day. She was distraught and I think, guilt-stricken, that Rosemary "had been living in such squalor." I told her I had offered to help her find a nice apartment but she refused. She hadn't seen her sister in ten years. She said she'd found more than $1,200 hidden in her room, that she knew I had been helping her all those years and that she and Bob, her husband, wanted to "do something for me." I told her that Rosemary had already taken care of me and I told her about our joint account and the inheritance from Kay Blizzard, whom she knew. She said "fine, you keep that money. I have her trust fund." I never knew how much was in the trust fund; never asked, not my business, but my boss knew and he told me it was a lot. I wish Rosemary had been able to spend it on herself and have a better life than she did at the end.

I let a year go by before I closed the account and transferred the $40k to an IRA. And there it sits, almost twenty years later. I haven't spent a penny of it, don't need to and I don't intend to if I don't have to. I'm not much of a spender. I like the feeling of security the money has given me. It's there if I need it.…Rosemary and I did well by one another. We couldn't have a truly authentic relationship because of her illness but I did the handsome thing by her and she rewarded me handsomely in return. May she rest in peace.

Avesa and Jeremy.

CHAPTER 8

The Wedding

Thursday, August 19, 2004

E ly, Minnesota: The wedding party arrived late last night at the Blue Heron B&B. It was a cool, gusty night, with the silvery smell of wet birch in the air, clouds racing high overhead. We weren't in New Mexico anymore and this place was strange and wonderful. Ves and Jer drove up in their Suburu loaded down with stuff for the wedding, followed by Jer's parents, Sandy and Vince, then Dave and me in the new Camry with Tib in the backseat. We'd all had dinner in Two Harbors at a cute teahouse. Dave ordered walleye and I wish I had: he gave me a taste and it was delicious. We intend to eat all the walleye we can while we're here, it is a total treat. The drive up was dicey with the threat of a deer bounding out in front of the car at any moment .....then there was "Moose Alley" as Jer called it. We were on high alert and at the same time exhausted from the grind of flying in to Minneapolis that noon. There were no other cars on the road; we were headed to a place that calls itself "The End of the Road." We had all gathered in Duluth at Ves and Jer's new apartment, an old pre-WWI duplex sided with flouncy, flamingo pink shingles. Their spacious, high-ceilinged apartment took up the entire first floor. It was touching how homey and comfortable they had made their new place in such a short time. Ves took me out on the back porch to show me their view of Lake Superior. This was our first meeting with Sandy and Vince: Sandy is a little older than me with a kind, placid Midwestern face belying a restless energy. Vince looked like an old testament prophet with a full head of wild white hair and beard. He has that slight remoteness of the deaf, although I found out that he could hear pretty well one on one, and he later told me some good stories about his boyhood growing up on a farm, plowing with horses. He seems to have a good, kind heart like Sandy. Their lab, Abby, was a constant companion over the next five days; I think she connected with everyone, especially Tib.

We said good-night and settled in to our very clean and well-appointed rooms. The decor is north woods rustic, log walls and pretty quilts, little curls of birch bark and river stones for decoration. Breakfast this morning was scrumptious - scrambled eggs, bacon, fruit and delicious risen biscuits. It's just the eight of us for now (including Abby); the rest of the Kershaw clan is due in later in the day. Ves dissolved into tears at the breakfast table, anxious about all the things that needed to be done. She looks thin and stressed out; we all felt for her. We assured her it would all work out, not to worry, this is traditional bridal nerves, but she was really embarrassed and apologized several times for 'losing it.' Like we all haven't a million times! After breakfast we went for a walk on woodsy trails around the property with several bounding dogs. Ves & Jer went for a canoe ride, although it was very windy. Dave and I got in only one short canoe ride the whole time because of the fitful weather.

Ves' best friend Jen, her dad Rob and brother Chris joined us that night at a steakhouse in Ely. Jen looks great, sleek and healthy. Chris has matured a lot from the fidgety boy I met in San Francisco a few years ago, Rob, the dad, is a character, very much the outgoing Leo. They're camping near the wedding lodge, Kawishiwi. The rest of the San Francisco posse arrives tomorrow and will stay on a houseboat pulled up near the lodge.

Friday, August 20, 2004

Jer's brother, Mark, a sentimental but jokey guy (a cartoonist) and his wife, Anna, who has the most soothing, mellifluous voice, and silent teenage son, Hans, join us at breakfast this morning. It will be great to get to know them over the next four days. Breakfast flows into lunch and we all meet at the Chocolate Moose in Ely for a bite. Along comes Smith and boyfriend, Christopher. Smith will videotape the wedding. We all have a great chat before taking off for separate pursuits. Dave and Tib drove up and down every street in Ely to look at the homes that had been brought in from other defunct mining towns. Dave commented that he couldn't find the barrio. Ves and I head out to a hiking spot, Bass Lake, I think, very pretty trails around a lake. We meet up with Smith and Christopher. I hike for a while with Christopher who is a very interesting guy my age. He works in screenwriting and acting and earns a living, I heard from Ves, with walking tours around North Beach and China Town. Ves and I do the last half of the hike together, chatting away, the only time we have alone for the entire five days. Not that I'm complaining: occasions like this that bring together so many friends and family are rare and to be prized. Around 3:00, Ves and I head back to Kawishiwi for the wedding rehearsal after which the whole party reunites in Ely at the Chocolate Moose for a dinner. Everyone turns up: Marv, Mary, the boys, Debbie Anderson, Elizabeth, Selene, Jer's whole family, the posse from San Francisco (Kate & Dav, Jake, Collette, Jen, her folks, Danny, Cora & Alan, did I forget anyone??). Marv supplies lots of good wine and the party heats up, ending with a campfire on a beach near town.

Saturday, August 21, 2004

This is the big day, Ves and Jer's wedding day !!! It's bright and calm. Summer in Ely, they say, has been cool and rainy but today it's full hot summery. Everyone is keyed up at breakfast. I'm feeling nervous and can only imagine how Jer and Ves must feel. They give us all the briefing on the assignments for the day. The level of organization that Ves and Jer have brought to this wedding is impressive, and Jer is involved every step of the way, which he demonstrates when we arrive at his former boss' house to pick flowers. He and Ves have thought out the flowers to the smallest detail which Jer relates: no goldenrod because some guests are allergy-prone, pick small flowers for the cake, showy flowers for the bouquet. We go over the large garden which Jer seems to know well as he points out different flowers that would work well. He even has thoughts on the fleabane (a favorite of mine!). He leaves Tib, Dave, Anna and me to work all morning picking flowers, mostly black-eyed susans and arranging them in ten mason jars weighted down with stones gathered from Lake Superior shores and decorated with ribbons. I set aside the nicest flowers for Ves' bouquet and Anna finds the sweetest little johnny-jump-ups for the cake. After we finish, we return to Kawishiwi Lodge where the others have been setting up tables, with linens, wine glasses, cutlery and china. It looks fabulous, the contrast between the rustic wood of the lodge and the elegant tables is stunning. Dave gets a fire going in the big stone fireplace and we wrap twinkle lights around the huge vigas. Finally, we finish and everyone heads back to the Blue Heron to get dressed for the wedding. I quickly dress and run up to knock on Ves' door; Jen is helping her dress. She looks so beautiful in her gown; Dave is knocked out when he sees her. We play that funny game of keeping Jeremy from seeing her until they meet near the bridge over the little stream leading to the Lodge. The wedding party assembles and walks over the bridge and down the hill and around to the place near a grove of tall trees. A tent has been set up in case of rain, but we won't need it today. Ves and Jer walk between the column of guests down the hill, followed by the Irishman Michael playing a solemn tune on his fiddle. We all form a large circle facing one another. Marv steps forward into the circle and gives the welcome to everyone. He's followed by Vince who reads from the Bible about the nature of love; Corinthians I think. He steps back and I come forward to talk about the meaning of marriage, ending with a poem by George Elliot: "What greater thing is there than for two human souls to feel that they are joined together / To strengthen each other in all labor / To minister to each other in all sorrow / To share with one another in all gladness / And to be with one another in the silent, unspoken memories." Then I said, "Ves and Jer will now begin their vows." They face one another holding hands, Ves goes first and what she said was so moving and heartfelt. I don't think there was a dry eye in the circle. Jer was fighting to maintain control, just a few tears sliding down his cheeks from the side of his eyes. Then he said his vows; telling Ves how much he loves her. When he finished, Jen came forward with the rings, saying that the rings were tied with a ribbon; she would pass them around the circle for each person to hold for a moment and give the couple their blessing. When the rings had gone around the circle, Jen untied them and Ves and Jer slipped the rings on one another's fingers and kissed. Sandy stepped forward to present the couple and give the blessing, sending them out to make a life together. They lead the way up the hill, Michael fiddling behind, to start the reception line. Ves' brothers (Alec, Kieran and Will) start popping the champagne and pouring under the tent as the photo session goes on with every possible combination of family and friends posing with the couple. We go in to dinner and feast on pecan encrusted walleye with wild rice and salad. The wine is flowing and toasts begin, Jer's brothers and Ves' girlfriends have us all laughing and crying. Dave wants to read his much-rehearsed cowboy poem, Jack Potter Courtin' but he's clutching, whispering to me that the timing is just not right. Marv gets wind of this somehow and works on Dave, urging him to do it; if he doesn't, he'll always regret it. Dave lets the toasting time slip by and then it's time to go outside so the crew can clear the tables to make the dance floor. Outside, Dave finds the sweet spot for his poem. As everyone gathers around for another champagne toast, he begins with the story that Ves told us on Christmas morning about Jeremy's proposal: how she knew he was going to propose when she felt the little box in his jacket pocket as she took his arm and how nervous he was. Then Dave read his humorous poem and everyone laughs at the punch line: "Says Jack, now this here pony - is he mine or is he ours? / Our pony, Jack !, she answered, and her voice was soft as moss / Then Jack, he claims he kissed her - but she claims he kissed the hoss!"

Back inside for the dance party, led off by Ves and Jer. It was so much fun, almost everyone got up to dance, small children, old folks, even the Lutherans. I think Tib danced every dance; I think I did too. It was the best of times. I talked to so many people that I hadn't seen in years and even got tricked again by Debbie Anderson. Ah, nostalgia. Dave and I agree that the wedding was one of the highlights of our lives. It had traditional elements yet was fresh and creative and was just so perfectly Avesa and Jeremy.

The next day is a barbecue/clean-up at the lodge, followed by dinner at the Blue Heron prepared by our curmudgeon chef of the wedding dinner. We all say good-bye the next day. Tib goes with Sandy and Vince to the Minneapolis airport; Dave and I take off to visit Tom Halstead in Marcell on Turtle Lake. Mark said it best: as he walked by me tearfully, "I hate for this to be over." Amen, brother. We are filled up from this wedding; we are full.

Esme and baby Silvi aka Nuie or Nubers

CHAPTER 9

The Esme
and
Silvia Journal

Thursday, June 28, 2007

We have a baby !! Jer called at 6 a.m. to tell me that Esme Marie was born at 3:35 a.m. She weighted in at 8 pounds, 3 ounces and was 19 inches long and is VERY cute. Ves had a bit of rough time at the end, pushed for three hours to no avail, and finally they had to use suction which Jer said was really scary, he though they were going to suck the baby's brains out and she does have a big hematoma from it. I hope she's okay; Jer thinks she's alright from it. He said that Ves was magnificent and did it all naturally the way she wanted to. I'm going to go pit the cherries from my tree now to dry them to send to Ves like she asked me to. Now I know how to finish the story quilt, I'll put in a sun and a 3/4 moon like it was last night and for the bird, maybe a stork carrying a basket with an "e" on it.

Friday, June 29, 2007

Talked to Ves a long time last night and she told me the whole story. She was blacking out between pushes, exhausted, and that's when they used the suction. Esme is fine though. Ves said Jer broke down sobbing after it was over, he was so scared. I was all weepy and emotional yesterday all day too. I guess I didn't realize how anxious I was about her giving birth. Risky business.

Thursday, July 5, 2007

Ves told me a cute story about Esme. Vince and Sandy drove up just for a day to see the new baby (they'll be moved there this Monday !!) Jer was holding her and whipped open her little shirt, saying "babies gone wild !" Well Esme gave him the dirtiest look and held the frown for quite a while. We have a picture of it. So funny. Ves says she has a lot of funny little looks. Only three weeks to go and we'll see her in person.

Sunday, July 9, 2007

Talked to Ves last night and heard Esme's voice for the first time. She was hungry and it sounded like she was growling. What a little tiger ! I had her chart done and am studying it. Quite a complex person ! Gemini Rising with Moon conjunct Jupiter in Sag in opposition right on the cusp of the 7th House. Wow. We got a party girl. Venus conjunct Saturn in Leo in the 4th house is kind of troubling, although my book says it is the sign of an artist. I'm just going to give Ves little bits of it at a time. She told me Marv and Mary visited yesterday - they drove all the way up from Mpls just for a two hour visit - and Mary asked Ves if I had had Esme's chart done yet. I'm going to keep it on the downlow.

September 18, 2007

I never did get around to writing about our trip to Duluth and falling in love with the Es. The weather these days is so beautiful I don't want to be inside at all to write. She's only six weeks old but smiling ! I did choo choo with her little legs and said, "look, it's Kicky Kershaw." She looked surprised and did a big slow smile. She's going to be a pistol!! My best memory of many memories is taking her into bed with me once in the early morning so poor exhausted Ves could get some sleep. I snuggled her in right under my arm and we both snoozed off. She woke up a few times and started to fuss but dozed right off again after I made some comforting animal murmurs.

October 20, 2007

Got back on Wednesday from a five-day visit to Duluth to see Ves, Jer and Esme, who is 3 ½ months old now and the most delightful baby ever born (indulgent smiles here for the proud grandmother). She remembered me ! They picked me up about 10:30 after spending the evening visiting Vince and Sandy. Es was half asleep but when I put my hands on her and said her name, she woke right up, got all excited and smiled and smiled. She was clearly glad to see me !! I could hardly take my eyes off of the irresistible Es the whole time I was there. She's so pretty with silky peachy skin - as my old aunts used to say, 'she looks good enough to eat'!! (Ves had a crazy dream about fried green tomatoes and dredging Es in egg and flour, stopping just before she put her in the frying pan). She is always smiling in this really charming way, sometimes with a little shoulder wiggle that is adorable, and she's obviously very bright. She seems to know what books are all about and gets this look of concentration looking at the page, then just explodes in excitement, waving her arms and legs and doing a little baby shout. Once I took her hands in mine and got my face in close to hers and fervently said "I love you". Her eyes got all big and dark and she lifted her face towards mine and sort of went 'oooohh.' She got it - I know she totally got it! I did the alphabet song several times with her - I made it up, it's all the letters sounded out to the tune of "Barbara Anne." She would listen intently and after the final zee, zee, zee, zee, give a big smile and leg kick. Ves and Jer are such good parents, just the best. I'm so happy to see Ves all relaxed and enjoying the baby and nursing after the rocky start they had with the thrush. Marv came up on Saturday to take us out on his boat and to spend the night. Ves made a nice dinner, and we sat around the table afterwards, reminiscing about the old days in Jackson Hole and what happened to this old friend and that. Es was sitting on Jer's lap facing out, looking at each person's face in turn talking, taking it all in with her dear little face just shining. It's just amazing to me that she's so sociable and engaged at her tender age. It's going to be wonderful to see her grow up. The next time I see her in January, she'll be 6 months old and beginning to eat solid food and sitting up by herself. When I was just there, I'd get her to wrap her 'finnews' around my two index fingers and she would try really hard to pull herself up and look very proud when she made it. She did it right too by bracing her lower back and not rounding her back. She's really strong for her size - if you put your hands under her armpits, she'll stand up for a long time with her knees locked . Jer did a photo shoot on the story quilt. She was on her tummy in a turtle pose and for a brief second it looked like she was going to roll over onto her back. Jer and I both gasped !! I'm sorry that I won't see every step forward she makes, but I do hope to get up there at least every three to four months so that I won't miss too much.

Monday. January 21, 2008

Ves and Es arrived on New Year's Eve for a week and it was the best, despite the terrible cold I had ! We had a party for them and Es got lots of gifts. Ves is such a great mom and I love her mom voice! Esme is just delightful, so sociable for a six-month old, almost ready to start crawling. She's adorable....I love that baby!! I got to give her the first bite of mashed banana. Ves and I were feeding her rice cereal and I put in a dab of the banana. Es stopped cold, looked at me stunned and then got really excited, waving her little arms around. The birth of a foodie.

Wednesday, February 27, 2008

Back from the trip last night (and did catch a cold that seems to be going away rapidly now that I'm home !) I just spent almost a week with Esme (8 months old tomorrow), Ves and Jer, and it was a wonderful time, so many great memories. She's just a beautiful baby, a pink and plump cherub, but strong as an ox for her size. Esme's doing lots of new things like crawling, standing and trying to talk. She made great strides while I was there, pulling herself up to a standing position against her toy piano. She learned to get her feet together and started sidling sideways....I bet she'll be walking within a month. Sandy says that Jeremy was walking at 8 1/2 months. I think she'll be talking early too. She's trying out all kinds of sounds – a very emphatic 'Da Da Da' packed with feeling was big and also 'Esth Esth'. Can it be she's trying to say her own name?

I wish I had a picture of the expression on her face when I did the fake phone call routine (many times over!). She'd be in her high chair playing with measuring cups and I'd pick one up and put it to my ear: "brnnnng, brnnnng, Hi ! Oh hi ! how are you ? (bright and phony voice) then I'd make some small talk ending with "Yes, yes, Es is here …would you like to talk to her? Okay, here she is…" then I'd say "it's for you, Es" and put the "phone" up to her ear and she would look just thrilled. After I did this a dozen times over the week I was there, she finally gave me a look that was priceless, like 'oh you faker, how dumb do you think I am?'

I took care of her all one day - the works, feeding, diaper changing, naps. I was a little nervous about being up to the task after 35 years !! I was feeling really lousy that day with the cold so I lay down on the sofa after I put her in her cradle and we both fell asleep for two hours. I woke up when I heard her moving and we both lay there having the nicest conversation looking up at the ceiling. We did fine with the day.

Saturday night Ves, Es and I went to the "Feast of Nations" night at UMD – a buffet dinner and amateur night put on by the foreign students assn. We sat off to the side of the stage about 20 feet from the performers, and Esme, who had been sitting quietly before the singing and dancing started, just came alive. She waved her arms and legs and loudly tried to sing. I think more people were watching her than the performers on the stage. When a quiet ballad number came on, Ves had to take her to the back of the room, she was so rowdy.

Sunday, April 20, 2008

Talked to Ves and could hear Esme in the background growling and making monster noises. Ves says she's a food monster now. Also she's pulling herself up onto the kitchen chairs and pushing them around. Can't wait to see them on May 20.

May 20 – 29, 2008

Esme turned 11 months while I was there and I saw her take her first two steps. It was a big moment. She stands a lot now independently and she can get to her feet very fast when she wants to - like when she's in the playpen out on the porch and someone goes by on the sidewalk. She's a minute away from walking. When she would fall from standing, onto her rear end, I would say 'Kaboom' and she'd always laugh her cute little baby laugh - that girl's got a sense of humor. She was trying hard to talk, saying 'mama' and – I'm not making this up – 'bwabwa' for me – and also not making it up – 'yum' for dinner (after much coaching). Jer really wants to be called papa but he's getting called mama for now. Ves and Jer think that 'mama' is the all purpose word for anything she wants.

It was wonderful to spend ten whole days with Esmarie, as Jer calls her, beginning with the bath in the morning to the raucous time on the sofa at night. She's almost outgrown her bathtub, Ves tells me she's at something like the 95th percentile for height for her age. She has the cutest sturdiest rosy pink little bod, very strong. She's eating a lot of solid foods now although Ves and Jer are cautious about giving her just anything, especially spicy foods. Her favorite foods are yogurt, hands down, pureed carrots and lots of cheerios. Ves tells me she loves homemade pea soup and is crazy for Popsicles. I offered her some chocolate and butterscotch gelato when we were out on a walk and she didn't like it at all, no doubt about that with the shivers and faces. After breakfast, we'd go for a walk either with Ves carrying her in the sling or if Ves had a meeting at school, I'd take her on the lake walk for a few hours in their wonderful all terrain stroller. As soon as the stroller started rolling, Es would go into 'Buddha mode' as Ves calls it, then off to sleep for the morning nap. After lunch, she'd play for a few hours and she plays alone very well, sometimes in Sandy's play pen that she likes a lot - which was surprising to me since Ves hated a playpen when she was Es' age.

While I was there Esme took a liking to a new doll someone gave her, all plastic with vinyl hair that Ves named Ethel (or is it Ethyl?) There was some doubt as to whether she should have this doll at all since she puts everything in her mouth. But this too shall pass and quickly, I think. I spent a few afternoons with her out in the backyard, and she'd always make a beeline to the garden where she would start out by ripping leaves from plants, much to Vesa's distress. Then she would pick up handful after handful of dirt and just feel it between her thumb and fingers. She moved on to the rocky bed under the juniper by the back steps (and she knew just where she wanted to go too, crawling rapidly). There she put many larger stones into her mouth (no choking issue there) and rubbed them on her two bottom toofers, tasting them and then threw them down. After about a dozen of these stones, she stopped putting them in her mouth and started just tossing them back into the bed. This was an intense experience for her. She did that deep breathing thing that babies do when they're learning something new.

The best time of the day was sofa time after dinner. That's when Es really turned it on, amped it up, shrieking, laughing and carrying on. She's very ticklish. One night, Jer left the sofa to work on his computer at the kitchen table. Es wanted him back and flung her arm out to him from the sofa, calling 'mama, mama' rather commandingly. There was no doubt she wanted her Papa back on the sofa. We noticed that she wants everyone to be together in a sociable way. Ves told me that a few days after I left she took Esme to the playground and swung her in the baby swing. Es watched a group of older kids playing nearby and called out to them to come play with her. Amazing for a one-year old !!

New slang I learned from Avesa (and I've been learning new stuff from her lo these many years as I'm sure she will from Es): Upon wiping Es' face with a wet cloth, Es protesting: "Sorry to harsh your mellow, Es."

Wednesday, October 22, 2008

But back to Duluth and the delightful 8 days I got to spend with the Es (Ves and Jer too of course). Esme is now 15 months old and just the most rollicking, fearless little daredevil of a toddler. She stormed the steps of the corkscrew slide and I had no choice but to follow her up but I was too scared to go down it and had to carry her back down. Ves went down with her on her lap and even Ves said it was scary but Es was thrilled, hair flying and all excited. Her walking is steady and fast, she's almost running. In fact, when we went to the park I would take her down from the stroller, and I had to be ready to run to keep up with her. Funny how she goes into "Buddha mode" as Ves calls it when she's in the stroller, but the minute she's out she's moving and 'talking' the whole time. I would hook a finger in the hood of her jacket to keep track of her and push the stroller with the other hand…it worked out well ….and when we got to the dell, I'd turn her loose to run down the long slope of grass. Then she would head for the stage and then out the back and down the steepish hill to the stony beach. She'd go up and down this hill several times, constantly picking up things to roll around in her fingers and hold onto. Such energy !! The idea was to 'hot walk' her, as Jer says, to tire her out so she would nap. She's almost ready to talk, speaking in gibberish with lots of expression and meaning. Es definitely understands a lot – if you ask her 'where's your belly button? 'where's your nose? she points to it. And she also knows what's not English – in her highchair at lunch, I'd say something like 'tu comida esta sabrosissima !" or "das schmeckt, ja?" and she would give me a look of wonder and smile with delight. And what was amazing…..Es was playing in her toy box and I said to Jer 'what is Baby Einstein all about? I saw that in Es' toybox yesterday ….and then jokingly, I said to Es, "would you bring me that Baby Einstein DVD.? And she promptly dug it out and brought it to her Dad !!! Ves and Jer have been teaching her sign language to use before she begins talking, but she hasn't really picked it up. Then she started doing this sign, pointing her right index finger at her left palm, sort of like 'time out.' None of us could figure out what it means. We think it might mean that she needs her diaper changed. On the changing table, I did the sign to her, and she smiled mischievously at me, like she was enjoying a little joke. Ves says maybe she thought I was signing that I needed my diaper changed !

Did I mention what a hard worker she is? We would walk down the yard to the compost pile and she would insist on carrying the bucket even though it was pretty heavy sometimes. She loves to pick tomatoes and raspberries in the garden, and helped me gather what was left in the garden. Ves warned me, and I watched carefully to make sure she didn't put a cherry tomato in her mouth but what she did was nibble on it with her front toofers and then suck on it, nibble and suck some more until she got it down to a small piece. What a kid ! Can't wait to see them all again at Thanksgiving.

P.S. from Avesa:

"I forgot to tell you that the other night (less than an hour after you asked "did you ever figure out what the finger sign meant?" Es and I were upstairs getting ready for bed and she picked out some books to read, among them the baby signing book. I opened it on a random page and you won't believe it, but it said, "some babies sign "more" not the correct way, but by pointing their index finger into their palm." So there you go!

Monday, December 8, 2008

We had our Thanksgiving dinner on Friday with Sandy and Vince, Sean and Tim, Aiden and Gracie, and of course Ves, Jer and Esme. It went really well – other than the smoke alarm going off from the turkey at one point – but - we pulled it off beautifully in the end and it was a delicious dinner with good cheer and cooperation all around. Ves did a wonderful brined turkey, a sausage stuffing and two kinds of cranberry sauce, Jer made an apple/cranberry pie with vodka crust, I made the Jack Daniels sweet potatoes with apricots, Sandy the mashed potatoes and rolls, Dave the stringbeans. Even though Miss Miss had a cold, she was in good spirits, the rowdy, happy toddler. As Ves warned me and I quickly found out, she will not get into her stroller anymore, which is tough because it was so cold for walking with her outside. When you try to force her into the stroller, she throws herself backward and then goes all limp when you try to pick her up then all stiff and unbending when you try to get her to sit in the seat. So we set off walking instead and she wants to explore the neighbor's backyards – kind of embarrassing – eventually you have to lead her away, like when she's knocking at some stranger's door, and then she pitches a little fit and goes limp, so a few times I had to just pick her up and carry her away like a package under my arm. The classic toddler tote. She didn't mind that at all though; she quieted right down!

One of my favorite images of Es is her hunkering down on her haunches like an asian peasant and turning things over in her hands intently concentrating, making the duck lips while making this growly clearing noise in the back of her throat. Jer told her she won't have any friends if she continues doing that. She also will stand for a long time and expertly flip through magazines and catalogs with her thumb. She loves catalogs just like her Baba did at her age! I think it's quite a sight to see.

I wonder if she's going to be a soccer girl – she got Dave and me to play ball with her every day and she is a real toughie. When she falls down, she doesn't cry but groans with frustration. She only cries when she really gets hurt to the level of a bruise. I say this - yet - she also really seems to like the girly stuff, e.g., I bought a new tube of Burt's Bees pomegranate lip gloss. She watched with rapt attention as I applied it, then I put it on her - with her insisting - and she received it as though it were the sacrament. She's watched me put on 'my face' (Ves tells me it's the same with her) and her eyes are big and awed-looking as she watches.

And the piano ! We all – Vince, Sandy, Sean, Tim, Ves, Jer, Dave, me and the three kids Aiden, Gracie and Esme drove out in three cars to the boonies the day after our Thanksgiving to cut Christmas trees. Dave was really silly with Aiden and got him giggling pretending to be attacked by a tree and trees running away, etc. That night we decorated while playing Christmas music – it was SO fun and such a happy occasion. During one jazzy tune, can't remember which, Es ran over to her piano and tore off a riff that fit right in with the music and carried it on even - and she did it with such verve and dash! Ves and I both caught it and couldn't believe it. It was phenomenal !! And she did it with her whole body, not just her fingers, it was a total body-English thing. I'll never forget it....it was really startling.

Thursday, January 22, 2009

The girls left one week ago and what a wonderful time we had ! We went to Santa Fe on the train to visit Hillary and Alana, went with Dave to the aquarium and Biopark on a spectacularly beautiful winter day, and we had friends over (Jess, Avery, Barbara P., as well as Will, Dan and Jane) for lunches and dinners and a picnic with Tib at the park. Ves loved the aquarium and Biopark – had never seen it before. Es enjoyed the kid's fantasy garden, heck we all did, walking inside the giant pumpkin, the ant maze and under the big buzzing fly. Es went down the scary slide several times and Dave zoomed her around in her stroller making silly car sounds. Afterwards we went to Lotaburger for lunch and Es had her first cheeseburger, fries and shake. She loved that shake and dipping her fry in a little cup of ketchup. She started doing this funny thing running in a crouch with her arms straight behind her palms up like she's a duck.

Will, Dan and Jane came over one night for dinner and Es was so adorable. When her bedtime came, she ran around the table giving everyone a goodnight kiss. I said, "you forgot Will !" and she ran all around the other way and gave him a kiss, much to his delight. She knew who he was! She is such a people person ...and a kitty person too! She got along great with Willie and June, started making 'yowl' kitty sounds to them and patting and squeezing them. June didn't mind a bit, he'd flop down in front of her and if she squeezed him too hard, he'd be right back for more. I noticed that Es is very compassionate – at the mall she saw a little boy crying and screaming and she got a really worried look on her face and said 'who dat?' She said several words clearly much to Avesa's surprise: "apple, cat, dog, Dave, Ba, bath." She's going to be talking real soon. Ves and Es went down to Andra's overnight on Friday and had a fun time with Andra's girls. It was sad to see them go but there are lots of memories to treasure.

Wednesday, April 08, 2009

Been gone for ten days visiting Ves, Jer and Esme for my birthday. Ves and Es made me the most beautiful card. It's on blue paper that Esme finger painted and with a cutout picture of a mama polar bear & baby sculpture on front and sweet words of love inside. There was another Es fingerpaint work on the fridge and Es put up her arms to me in the kitchen to be picked up then she pointed (her finger pointing is just adorable) at her artwork and wanted to go over to it. She pointed to various parts and I could tell she felt really proud of it. Then she motioned that she wanted to look into the refrigerator so we explored the inside of the fridge for awhile. I took the caps off condiments and let her smell them. We went through the cheese drawer and the veggie drawer and investigated the leftovers. She really enjoyed it.

I watched Es when Ves was at work and we had such a good time. She's not talking in sentences yet – she's now 21 months old – but she does speak volubly in what sounds like Navajo with an occasional English word thrown in, like 'apple, cool (pronounced with two syllables 'coo-ul') baby, doggy, mama, cheese, ice, Da …and more. So funny at Alec's house the day I left - she got ahold of the cell phone, expertly flipped it open, put it to her ear and said "Hi" very briskly, then proceeded to pace the floor, talking away in a conversational tone, occasionally scuffing her heel or toe on the floor. Hilarious. The shopping trip to Target was a gem too. Jer went off with the cart and Es and I headed to the kid's section to look for gloves. On the way, she found a cute Hello Kitty bag and put it over her shoulder, then she flipped through the bathing suit racks and found a cute pink swim suit – in her size – and put that over her arm. Jer and

I had to sneak both items away from her at the check-out. Jer distracted her with helping him unload the cart. She likes to help. Nap time every day was a challenge. Es doesn't have the routine of being put in a crib at a certain time every afternoon to take a nap, consequently; nap time is a free form event. Ves tells me that everyone gets her down differently, but; the one constant with Es is that she has to have her body on yours to nap. Now this was a delightful experience really, once you could persuade her to nod off but that wasn't easy. We read every book many times (she really likes the Big Sister Little Sister best, followed by the Slide book, Five Little Monkeys and many others, although Goodnight Moon still has clout. We have to remember this Five Little Monkeys chant when Es starts to jump rope. ("Five little monkeys jumping on the bed, one fell off and hurt his head, momma called the doctor, , the doctor said," no more jumping on the bed" and so on from five to one.) The Big Book of Potty Training was really riveting and also a little horrifying to Es at the same time I think. She's beginning to use the potty, but with some resistance (Ves is right not to push it too hard). Finally Es would nod off and slump against my side or lay her sweet head on my lap. It was hard to move her without her waking up so I would stay with her and do my crossword puzzle.

We went to the old railroad depot to the Children's Museum one gray day. Es was right at home there, put on a knave's costume and then went to another room to armor up with shield and helmet. She took me over to the railroad museum which is very impressive. What a contrast, that tiny girl with her plastic medieval armor striding along like she owned the place next to those HUGE engines and railcars. It was unnerving. I saw disaster at every turn. I noticed that Es has good problem-solving abilities: the helmet was too large for her to wear, especially with the visor down, so she turned it sidewise in order to see which gave her a decidedly rakish look. Occasionally she got tired of wearing all this armor and would hand it off to me to carry for a while then would want it back. Another problem solving episode I saw Es perform was in the backyard after it snowed. We went outside with two big spoons and three plastic containers, two round and one oblong, to play in the snow (which mainly consisted of Esme eating the snow). At one point, she wanted to pick it all up and move it to another spot. She experimented with different groupings of the five objects until she found one that allowed her to carry it all at once. Ves says that this is a genetic Kershaw trait.

I taught Es to 'Eskimo kiss' by rubbing noses. She likes it a lot and will promptly rub noses when asked.

Ves called the other day to tell me that they received the Easter 'basket' I sent. It was a tissue lined box that I filled with cherry blossoms, arugula flowers, spearmint leaves and thyme. I put in two packets of seed – pumpkin and sunflower for Es – some foil-wrapped chocolate chickens and eggs and the magnetic letter and numbers that used to be Avesa's. Jer told me that he had been looking for them but couldn't find them to buy, so I'm glad I saved them ! Wish we could be with them for their Easter brunch and egg hunt but I will be there for Es' birthday on June 28.

Monday, April 13, 2009

....and here's what Ves wrote back:

Thanks, Barb, for writing such a lovely account of your time with Es. I will be sure to print it out and glue it into the book. Es and I went up to Ely last night to drive our friend Lara home (who found herself stranded in Duluth this week), and we had a wonderful time at her cabin drinking tea and dancing, then going to the local cafe this morning, where Es pushed herself into the middle of the local dude coffee klatch, found herself a seat beside them at the hearth (they were sitting in a circle of couches), with her plastic teacup full of water, and chatted it up, offering them bits of her muffin. It was amazing, Lara and I agreed as we watched from the sidelines. Some of the men agreed that we should be worried– what a flirt! She really likes Bernard, the French chef, remember him? It's late and I'm pooped– gotta make a big brunch tomorrow morning.

Here's an email I got from Sandy Kershaw today:

Thought I would share with you a moment with Esme and your picture. She has that collection of pics in the plastic sack in her toy box and she was sifting through them and couldn't find Baba. She became quite disturbed and dug around and looked at me and said Baba several times. I asked her if she lost Baba and she looked at me as if to say "yes and get crackin' to help me find her"! Sure enough Baba had fallen out of the sack and was at the bottom of the box. She was delighted to have her back and carried her/you around for several minutes! TRUE STORY!

July 13, 2009

The trip was fun and the Fourth of July party too. Marv has a beautiful big house and pool. There was a great spread of food, badminton which was really fun and swimming in the pool. Ves, Sandy and I took turns keeping an eye on Ezzie (that's what she calls herself). She's so much fun to be with...she loved the pool and kicked up a storm, something she learned in swim class at the Y this winter. Ves and Jer told her that I was coming to visit and would be there when she woke up on Thursday. So I was sitting on the bed talking to Ves who was doing her yoga thing on the floor and Es was still sleeping. Finally she got up and came in the room and froze when she saw me and whispered "It's Baba" with this look of fright on her face. She ran over to Ves and buried her face in Ves' neck. I had to laugh even if my feelings were hurt a little. She was over her fright in a few hours though and we had a really good time together. Ves and Jer took advantage of me being there to get a lot of things done around the house - I'd take Es to the playground or the lake walk in her stroller. She doesn't talk in sentences yet - although at one point during Marv's party, we went looking for Avesa and started climbing the stairs to Marv and Mary's bedroom and I swear to god, she said "Maybe she's up here." I couldn't believe my ears. She loves big words like "dangerous" and "ridiculous." Says them over and over. I'm told I was like that too. Her favorite word is "milk" meaning mama's milk and that's going away this week poor girl when Ves and Jer go on a five-day bike trip leaving Es with Sandy and Vince. Es doesn't want to give up being a baby and is resisting potty training too. Her birthday party was great, just the family and Ves' friend Brandy with her twin girls. We had bison burgers and a delicious fruit cake that Ves made with blackberries, blueberries, strawberries. The 'after party' was the best after everyone left. Es was really wound up, reveling, running around kicking the balloons and the soccer ball you gave her shouting "two years old!" That girl knows how to party! It's really something to see.

Here's an email I got from Sandy in reply to how it's going with Es at her house and Ves and Jer on their bike trip:

Hi, Barb. It is going well. She had a hard time getting to bed the first night. She was very hyper even with a 2 hr nap; I read to her but she just wouldn't settle down. I picked her up and she just burst out crying and asking for Mama. I asked her if she missed Mama and she wailed, YES. Then after comforting her I asked her if she wanted to go down stairs and watch a movie. She brightened up and within 10 min. of sitting in my lap she was asleep! She woke up cheery - looked over at us (with Abby in the bed, too) and said Hi! She and Abby are real pals. She feeds her each time and walks the driveway with her hand on Abby's back. Very sweet.

Today she didn't nap, but I think will go down okay. I think Ves and Jer did a good job preparing her. She asks about Mama and Daddy a lot during the day and I tell her that they are biking and that they will be back. That seems to satisfy her, She is so cute and smart – of course I could be prejudiced! I am typing with one hand because she is putting coins in my other hand from my Canadian money collection. She isn't indulged at all! Sandy

Wednesday, November 18, 2009

Back yesterday after ten days in Duluth watching Es for Ves and Jer while Sandy was away in Austin. I spent lots of time hanging out with Es as well as a lot of cooking and folding and a little ironing as well. I've been looking forward to this since the last time I was there.

The weather was warm and sunny most days, only a few days of rain, so we went outside for a lot of the day. She loved doing picnics. We packed a basket with food and a nice striped cloth. I let Es pick the picnic spot, three different spots actually. She said one day when I asked her what she wanted to do, "a long walk in the neighborhood." I asked "what is the neighborhood, Es?" She made a sweeping gesture to take in all that was out there. We set off down the alley. In one spot she likes, she pretended the space between two old telephone poles was her front door. I 'knocked' on the front door and she came around the pole saying "Hi ! This is Ezzy's house. Pleased to meet you." We played this game over and over until it was time to move down the alley looking for the gray cat that is as Ves says "insanely friendly" towards Es. We didn't see the cat and called for him and lo and behold, here he comes again running meowing with his big skunk tail so happy to see Es. I asked Ves later about the 'pleased to meet you" and she said that she and Jer taught her that. She is so funny with her definite "Yes" and equally definite "No please." Miss Miss knows exactly what she wants and what she does not

126

want at any given moment. We had one big struggle one afternoon at nap time. The routine is that Es puts on her 'napsuit' sometimes after a bath then gets a few books read to her then off to nap. When we went to put on the nap suit, she got out of her clothes quickly and then pulled off the diaper (not potty trained yet) and made it clear that she wanted to put her napsuit on without a diaper(I could tell she knew this was a no no.) I said no, you must put on a diaper. A wrestling match ensued and I succeeded in getting the diaper and the napsuit zipped on her but she was furious and bawling. I started pulling stuffed animals out of her basket and making each of them say DIAPER PLEASE ! After the fourth or fifth one, she started laughing. She has a good sense of humor. Another diaper incident – as I was changing a diaper, I told her it was really smelly and awful, time to use the potty, and she frowned at me and said "It's a nice one."

There was another terrible seizure when I was there. Es came down with a cold and ran a little fever on Monday morning, she was hot. Ves gave her some Motrin and by mid-morning, no fever and she seemed to feel fine. We went down to the Lake Walk and played on the "mountains" on the beach behind the bandstand then walked to the Food Co-Op for a snack, a huge blueberry muffin that Es devoured almost all by herself. She fell asleep in the stroller on the way home but woke up when we got home, ate a little lunch and acted fine. Ves took her upstairs for a late nap at 4:00 and within 15 minutes, Avesa called down to me in a terrified voice to bring the phone upstairs, to call 911. When I came in the bedroom, Ves was almost hysterical trying to get the cap out of this medication she had for emergency purposes; Es looked unconscious and had blue lips. It was horrifying. We turned her on her side and she vomited. I put my finger in her mouth back behind the teeth to open up her clenched jaws so the vomit could get out but Ves yelled at me to stop, that I shouldn't put my finger in her mouth. It was all very confusing and awful. She called 911 and within five minutes there were half a dozen EMTs crowding into the bedroom. By then Es had come around and was getting pink again. They advised us to take her to the ER which we did although all they can do really is to check to make sure she doesn't have an ear infection. This is her fourth or fifth seizure. Esme told me the next morning that she had had "a seizure and saw the doctor.' I asked her if the seizure hurt and she said 'no.' I really hope this is all resolved at four years old as is typical.

I sang her the alphabet song many many times and we watched the Dr. Seuss ABC video many times as well. She can sing it now with gaps. One day I said E-S-M-E spells Esme and M-O-M-M-Y spells Mommy y, D-A-D-D-Y spells Daddy. Her eyes got big and I could see the lightbulb went on. She got the connection between the alphabet and words. She's going to be reading at four I would bet. Before I came on this visit, Ama Sandy sent me some great pictures of Es. I wrote her back and commented on what a beautiful girl she is. Ama wrote back:

> *"She is not only a beauty but she is such an interesting child; she is caring, gentle, very curious, and very good in the fine motor skills (loves Vince's workshop) and is also very independent on most things. I just love her! It will be great to see you. We have been talking about your coming!"*

Ama is right ! She is a very caring and gentle little person. She pulled the chair up to the counter to help me make dinner. I was cutting warm onions and the tears were rolling down my cheeks. Es looked concerned and said "let me kiss and make better" and she did ! She is very sweet and affectionate with her Mom and Dad – and me too. At bedtime, I'd ask for a hug and she would rush at me and give me a big bear hug and kiss. As for the fine motor skills, I gave her a hard-boiled egg and told her to peel it and then she could eat it. She got to work with her little index fingernail and had the egg peeled perfectly in a matter of a few minutes and proceeded to eat the whole thing. I asked her if she wanted salt, she did, so I gave it a sprinkle as she ate it down. When she was finished, she said "more, please." I said we should try something else now and she was okay with that.

Halloween was just over when I got there and Es was still thinking about it. She looks pretty scared in the pictures that Jer and Ama sent !! At the end of the block near the Chester Creek stairs the Guerndt house has a very creepy scarecrow hanging on the side of the garage. Es wasn't afraid of it but fascinated. Every time we went down there she would stare at it for a long time. I asked her if she wanted to walk up to it by herself and she said solemnly "yes" and did. The next holiday is Thanksgiving which Jer, Ves and Es will spend in the Cities with friends and family but we will be in Duluth for Christmas and it will be so much fun !! Can't wait.

Sunday, November 29, 2009

Here's an excerpt from an email I received from Avesa today:

"Esme had a wonderful time calling the cats from every corner of the house and playing piano with Cora. Her language skills continue to explode, with more abstract self-descriptions like "I'm hungry" and "I'm not tired!" She napped a total of 1 hour over the past few days, stayed up late each night, jumping from one piece of Marv's hefty leather furniture to the next, yipping for joy. When we first drove up to his place on Wednesday night she declared, "What a nice house!" and the compliments continued as we went from one warmly lit room to the next.

On Thanksgiving morning we visited Mary's mother Mae in her nursing home, a clean and friendly facility west of downtown St. Paul on the "Indian Mound" bluffs. We went to several unfamiliar and charming neighborhoods this weekend, including Linden Hills, where we were following a friend's recommendation for Wild Rumpus, a quirky creature-filled children's bookstore, just a block from Lake Harriet.

Anyway, as we visited Mae in the hallway of her nursing home, she introduced the staff to our group of ten, and Esme then proudly announced, "This is my momma! and "I love my mama!" It was very sweet and slightly embarrassing. Jer walked with her as we left, taking a turn into the chapel on the ground floor. On the far wall above the pulpit, a carved wood Jesus smiled from his cross onto the pews and just as Jer was going to explain to her who he was, Es exclaimed, "That's a nice Daddy!"

However, I realized this weekend that she also uses the word "nice" to tame things that otherwise frighten her. Yesterday after we returned from shopping with Sean, the kids, and Ama and Pop Pop, we rushed back to Long Lake to get Es to take a nap during her usual time. No luck. After some unsuccessful sleepy time stories and lay-bys, I let her run upstairs into Marv and Mary's bedroom while Jer posted on his blog and Marv followed us up, wearing the trousers of Will's Halloween costume, a black hairy ape. Both Es and I watched him put the full mask over his head, slouch down, and then in perfect ape character, gallop toward us with his arms dragging at his sides. I jumped back, and seeing my alarm, Esme broke into hysterical screams, then sobs, even after Marv took off the mask, assuring her that it was just a Halloween costume. When he bent over to pull off the pants she screamed again, "No! No!" After she stopped heaving she left my lap and went back to touch the costume, now a heap on the floor, and declared, "That's a nice Halloween costume."

This made me recall her fascination a few months ago with the images of two Tyranasaurus Rexes in her library books. Each time I turned to those pages she would touch the paper and say, "He's nice!" even when I told her, "No, he's not that nice." At the time I joked that I hoped she wouldn't become one of those girls who tries to find the goodness in bad boys. The narrator of "Misguided Angel" from the Cowboy Junkies. Now I think her "Nice dinosaur" was more about self preservation and an innate understanding that she can conquer her fears by reframing the object in question. Mind over matter. I need to give her more credit."

Thursday, January 07, 2010

Dave and I arrived on the shuttle from the airport on the afternoon of the winter solstice. Monday, December 21. Esme gave us a big smile from her car seat in the back. Ves told us that they had been talking about us for several days to prepare her for our arrival. We stopped at the food co-op on the way home and Es demonstrated her compassion when I hit my head on the door getting back in the car and yelped, holding my head. I looked up to see a very concerned look on her face and she asked "Are you alright?" When we got to the house we carried the luggage upstairs and collapsed onto the bed exhausted. Es jumped up on the bed and got between us waving her mother out of the room with a "Go Mama, go away !! She settled down between us for a short while and then began to REALLY MISS HER MAMA and let out a big wail. Ves came right in and whisked her away for a nap. The next few days were a blur of activity getting ready for Christmas and Vince's 80th birthday party on the 23rd . I talked to Es a lot about Santa coming and sang Christmas songs. She seemed a little leery of it all, maybe because it follows so closely on the heels of Halloween which she may still be digesting …

Christmas Eve came with a blizzard raging outside but cozy inside with Ves' split pea soup for dinner by the twinkling lights of the ethnic Christmas tree (I added a Navajo lady doll to it this year). Earlier I'd read "Twas the Night before Christmas" from Avesa's old book with the beautiful finely-drawn illustrations. Es was into it and we topped that off with a singing of Rudolph the Red-Nosed Reindeer. After dinner, we put on Will Ferrell's movie, "Elf." which was hilarious. At the end, there's the classic image of Santa's sleigh traveling across the sky just under a full moon, THE SAME AS IN THE BOOK. I pointed this out to Es and she got it. She was definitely intrigued......

It was a classic Christmas in Duluth with heavy snowfall and traveling to grandma's house with the sleigh laden with gifts. Yes, we had to slog through a blizzard the last few blocks to Ama's house since the roads weren't plowed. Sandy made a wonderful Christmas breakfast followed by hours of opening gifts. Es got a lot of things she really liked, the favorite I think was the little shopping cart filled with toy groceries and the toy camping equipment with a real backpack. Then we were back to the house to get the beef bourguignon ready for Christmas dinner. Jer had rented a table to make room for everyone and despite the awful weather and snowy streets, they made it and a good time was had by all. Gracie and Es were so cute playing in Es' new tent, setting up their campsite. Es had her new Elmo along for the 'camp trip'. Ves pointed out that Es still loves her 'ride' the best and plays with it every day. In fact, if you want to find something that's missing, you can often find it in the trunk.

One morning at breakfast she sat at the head of the table flanked by Ves and Jer. She made a graceful motion of her head and arm toward each in turn and said "I love you Mommy" and "I love you Daddy." Then she looked at me and said "I love you Baba." However, she looked right at Dave and made no comment. I think his feelings were a little hurt ....but she doesn't know him as well as she knows me and she doesn't know me as well as she knows Ama, so that's the way it goes. He made a game up to play with her that she seemed to enjoy...perfect for a two-year old whose favorite word is NO ("no please" is out the window it seems) when she said 'no' he would said 'yes' until he got her to say 'yes' then he would say 'no.' It took her a little while to catch on, she had to think about it, so that was a good game. We had some fun times. She remembered the picnics of November and wanted to do it again in the snow. We packed up the basket with that nice striped cloth and some drinks and food and went out in the backyard and had a lovely picnic sitting on the ice benches alongside the path. For dessert we picked some delicious icicles from the garage and brought a bunch inside to make icicle soup. That was a big project with lots of stirring and pouring from one cup to another. Suddenly she noticed the icicles were missing and said "where's the icicles??" I said they melted and I could see an 'aha' moment happening. Later I heard her tell her Dad that "the icicles melted."

I'm looking forward to seeing Es again at the end of March. She changes so much every time I see her it's as though she's a new person. Right now she's into expressing her loving feelings towards everyone in her life. She knows that there's a new brother or sister coming this summer and her attitude toward the new baby is very sweet. She says emphatically, "It's a NICE baby" and asks her mother at random times "How's that baby doing?" Once she patted Ves' breast and said "Is the baby in there?"....It will be exciting !!

Thursday, April 01, 2010

I got back from a wonderful visit to Duluth on Tuesday night. Ves called the day before I left and said Es told her "I want to pick Baba up from the airport NOW !!! Everyone treated me so great for my birthday, Ves and Jer with presents, a funny card and a special dinner at Nakomis and Sandy and Vince with flowers, a lovely card and an incredible breakfast on Sunday morning. Esme has morphed into a new little girl, a slim elfin girl, just as cute as they come. She looks like a mini me of Sandy. She talks easily although with a slight stutter at times. She'll sometimes say "I I I I I …..want…".searching for the right word. We spent a lot of time together, mostly playing 'shopping.' She would pull out the table in her room from the wall, quickly and efficiently clear out all the clothes from her dresser and pile them up on the table with the toy cash register, scanner and credit card swipe. Isabel the baby doll and I would sit on the other side of the table and play customer. Es would pick up each piece of clothing and we would talk about it - the color, the fabric, whether or not it fit Isabel and then I'd say "how much" to which Es would reply "Two dollars" then I'd say "we'll take it, ring it up." She'd scan it and run the credit card and hand it over to me. I'd fold it and put it in the proper pile, saying "thank you Mr. Boy." She'd then say "you're welcome Baba !" I should explain at this point that Es is now a boy. She said to Jer one morning with a really touching earnestness: "Dad, you know I AM a boy." Jer looked a little alarmed but both he and Ves are taking this quite sensibly as a passing phase. She has 'boy clothes' and 'boy shoes' as well as 'wild clothes' (I think this all comes from Esme's current fascination with "Where the Wild Things Are") She wanted a baby brother but now she knows she will have a little sister and she has accepted this with good grace. When we went for a haircut, she said she told the woman she wanted a 'boy cut' – Ves jumped in and said she wanted something like a Christopher Robin cut. Es was the perfect customer, chatting away and got a beautiful cut, curving on the sides and layered very short in the back, really pretty. The haircutter asked her how old she was and Es promptly said "Two and a half" then looked around at the two men getting cuts on either side and made that graceful arm sweep that she does and said "we're all getting haircuts !!" It was adorable. The haircutter said she wanted to take Es home with her.

Ezzy is very sharp - I sang her Rudolph the Red Nosed Reindeer (her request) which ends with "he'll go down in history" so I asked Es if she knows what history is, not expecting an answer, and she says "it's a book." Holy Cow, she's only 2 1/2 years old and she knows that !!! I noticed that she's using a few new words she got from me - 'creepy' and 'amazing' come to mind. She's really funny....she chats non-stop with "you know, Baba...." and she knows exactly what she wants and does not want at any given moment. No guesswork there. She's the total two-year old with "no no no no no no" but despite all the toddler no no nos and tantrums, she is a very affectionate and loving little person, always telling her mom and dad that she loves them and when she says "I love you Baba" the heart melts. We did a lot of snuggling on the sofa watching the Curious George videos that I brought for her. When we played 'shopping' one day she just cracked up laughing, just a losing it type belly laugh. It was delightful

We stopped at the Olive Garden for soup and salad on the way to the airport. Afterward Ves went to the restroom and Ezzy and I waited in the lobby area. Es was running all over the place so I picked her up and we looked at the wine bottles along the wall. Es says "where's the beer?" I said "what ??" She says, "you know, the beer." I said "I don't know if they have beer here. Your dad wouldn't like to eat here then would he if they don't have beer?" And she says "Well.....no..." (the way she says 'well' is so cute) She's gotta be the cutest little kid on the planet. I'm sure going to miss her. Won't see her again now until the end of June for her BD. In the meantime I have a mental snapshot that I hold dear of Es in the bathtub, wet hair pushed back off her forehead and her face shining with joy.

Not included in the version I sent to Ves – I overheard Ves and Es talking before bed and Ezzy says to Ves "You're always leaving me" (Ves had just spent a long weekend in SF visiting her friends). Ves said "no, I'm not" rather defensively. The guilt curve ball at 2 ¾ years old !!

Avesa wrote:

"Es kind of blew my mind last night. I was going through photos, trying

to finish her first year album before the baby comes, and there was a pile of pics that you sent from your road trip to Four Corners a few years ago. Es picked up one of the cliff dwellings at Mesa Verde. She said, "This is from where you grew up!" and she said, "I've seen this, wait!" and ran upstairs, came back down with Marcia Keegan's book about two Pueblo Indian girls. She opened it to the page of Bandelier National Park and held the photo of Mesa Verde up to it. "Look, it's the same!"

Wednesday, June 23, 2010

Got in late evening and was thrilled with the fresh, pine-scented, cool air of Duluth. A very pregnant Ves picked me up – Es was asleep in her car seat. Ves looks great and while she says she has some low days, she was usually full of energy, upbeat and the picture of health. Es seems apprehensive about the new baby. She says things like "I want to be the baby !" She'll ask her mother "Do you love me?" and "I need a hug and a kiss." Poor girl ! (Later…Ves tells me that the Ezeroo is getting enthused and asks "what's the baby doing now?" She stuffed a small animal into her otter hand puppet, then pulled it out and said " the otter had her baby !") But back to the story…..got to the house at sunset and saw their beautiful fenced in yard. Es can now just go out the back door to play with no worries. Inside, I showed Ves, Jer and Es the clothes that Andra had sent, including many pairs of shoes that were most welcome and also the outfits that I had made. They all liked the blue calico dress and the hot pink polka dot outfit. In fact, Es picked it out to wear it several times in the coming week. The next day we went to Bug Camp held at a nature center and taught by a lively young woman aptly named Joy. The task that day was to go out into the wetland and capture bugs with a net. Jer snagged a baby salamander which was the big hit. The next and final bug camp was the next morning. Ves went this time. It was a gray and foggy day and Esme didn't want to go. The task was to build a bug house out of milk cartons then go out and find bugs to populate it. This wasn't so successful. Es was not at all interested in the bugs or the other kids and kept wandering off on her own. Sandy once said it best. "she's not a trained bear."

Saturday arrived and Jer was off work for the weekend. We went to an arts and crafts fair at Park Point that was fun. When it was time to leave, Ves and Jer went to get the car, leaving me with Es who took off running to the playground. I ran after her but she can run much faster than me so I kept yelling, 'stop, wait' which she did just until I caught up with her, then she would giggle and run off again. Finally we got to the playground and I caught up with her. I tried to pick her up and she threw herself on the sand backwards. Jer showed up at that point and carried her back to the car. I sat next to her in the backseat and said "you're a teaser, Es." She was incensed and said "no, I'm not" then asked "what's a teaser?" Ves explained that it's kind of fun and kind of mean. Es hotly denied being a teaser. Later, I heard her tell her Dad, "Baba, called me a teaser." I am not a teaser, I'm a nice girl !" Then a few days later, she came up to me frowning and said "Baba, I am not a teaser." This really got under her skin !! Ves told me that was the first time anyone had applied a label to her, and she did not like it.

Sunday was Esme's third birthday party. Funny, last year she said over and over "two years old!" and then later in the year she told everyone she was "2 ½ years old" but now she does not want to say "three years old." I wonder why. … Ves invited a bunch of people and we had quite an ambitious BBQ to put together – fajitas, guacamole, and all the fixins for that plus a beautiful berry cake. The guest list included Sandy, Vince, Aidan, Brandy and her twins, Jer's friend Charlie and his daughter, and two couples who were colleagues of Ves from school. Esme had a great time and got lots of nice gifts, among them a scooter bike from her parents, a swimming pool and sleeping bag from Vince and Sandy and

Marv and Mary, and a sticker book and a Dora the Explorer puzzle book from me that she liked a lot.

The rest of the week was really nice, on sunny days, we went to the park and along the lake walk. One hot steamy day we went to Chester Creek just two minutes from the house and splashed in a beautiful pool at the base of the prettiest waterfall. It was great to spend so much time with Ves and Esme together – only possible in the summertime. Next summer, everything will be very different with the arrival of the new baby.

The visit wrapped up with a trip to "Maryapolis," as Esme calls it, for Marv's annual Fourth of July party. Es was enthralled with her cousin Kier, who is a very handsome and sweet young man. I heard her chatting with him and saying "Baba has cactus at her house." She and Mary and I watched "Beauty and the Beast" before the party started. I was surprised at how good Esme's attention span is, she was totally engrossed. We all had fun in the pool and Ves and Es enjoyed visiting with all the cousins. Jer's brother Sean was there too with Grace and Aidan. A very good time. We drove back to Duluth in the early evening and got back just at dusk to see the fireworks show from the new balcony outside Ves and Jer's bedroom. Then to bed – we had to get up very early for the airport. Es gave me a very sweet hug and kiss to say good-bye.

NOW THE ESME AND SILVIA JOURNAL

Wednesday, September 22, 2010

Met Silvi for the first time tonight – the whole family picked me up at the airport just before bedtime. She was sleeping in her carseat – Es was wide awake and I was surprised at how much she's grown in three months! She wanted to see right away the presents I brought, just little things like a princess accessories set, puzzles and a memory game. The princess set was what she liked best. It consisted of a tiara, wand, ring and jeweled hair clip. Es, I found out is much more interested these days in playing pretend than in working puzzles. While I was there, she got into being a mermaid – she stuffed both her legs into one leg of a pair of white pantyhose, put on her bathing suit backwards and a pair of underpants on her head and declared herself a Mermaid, no name needed. She flippered all over the floor and bumped up and down the stairs. Then we watched 'Bambi' and she turned into Filene (sp?) who was Bambi's girlfriend and mother of his fawn. She found a brown velvet jacket and with black tights and she was Filene making 'thickets' all around the house. Really cute. Es loves her "little sis" (or 'lil gal") and hugs and kisses her, tucks stuffed animals around her head until her parents tell her to stop. If her mom or dad hold the baby too long, in her opinion, she'll say "okay, lil sis is happy now, you can put her in her bouncy chair now..." As for Silvi, she seems to be quite happy in her bouncy seat observing the world around her. She's a very calm, contemplative baby who loves getting her diaper changed. Sandy says she's never seen anything like it. Silvi loves the sweet 'kitty' talk and smiles and flirts. She tries to talk back, opens her mouth wide and makes sounds. On my last day, I had to pick Es up at her preschool at 11:45 sharp. At 11:25, I began putting Silvi into her sling and at 11:27, it began to pour rain. What to do? We couldn't all fit under my raincoat so I draped the hood of another raincoat over Silvi's head and she was completely covered. That good baby instantly went to sleep like a small bear against my chest and didn't wake up again until we had made it back to the house. Essie got her shorts wet and I was completely soaked but Silvi was warm and dry, maybe a little damp around the shoulders but she woke up all happy and ready to get back in her bouncy seat. Now I won't see them again until after Christmas when they come to visit us here in NM – can't wait !!

Saturday, January 8, 2011

Ves, Esme and Silvi visit – January 1-7, 2011

The house is so quiet since the girls left. I talked to Ves this morning and it was a mess in the Mpls airport going back - they got stuck there for five hours rather than the two hour layover they were expecting to get back to Duluth. She had a horrible time both coming and going. But she said they had a great time, lots of fun, and Dave and I thought so too. Ves said in the car last night that she was telling Jer all about it and Es kept piping up with things like "I ate a hot dog at an Indian's house." We went to the Indian dances at Santo Domingo Pueblo on Thursday. All the pueblos install their new governors and war chiefs on January 6 - they have a cane given to them by Abraham Lincoln and they pass it on that day. So when we got there we watched the tail end of one dance (this out in the open in the plaza - we brought folding chairs) Then the outgoing officials came in (dressed like Japanese – who knows why - one man was dressed up in a pink satin kimono like a geisha). They had the passing of the cane ceremony and shaking hands etc. Then another dance crew came in - at least 100 dancers doing the buffalo dance and a big crowd of drummers and singers alongside. Essie's eyes were big and she stuck real close to her mama. Last year I gave her a photo book about two pueblo girls and Ves says she's been really into it. So we watched the whole dance that went on for about an hour. Then they filed out and we got our chairs put together and were getting ready to leave when this Indian man came up and introduced himself as the new governor and asked us to follow him back to his house to join in the feast. (turns out he is a friend of Alana's from the Santa Fe Indian School, David Garcia) His house was full of people and a big table loaded with food and ladies bustling around waiting on everyone. The idea is you find an empty chair and eat then get up to let someone else sit down. We went in to the living room afterwards where all the women were sitting with the cane and men would come in to pay their respects and sprinkle corn meal. Ves, Silvi and Es found seats and chatted with the women. Es told me that day was her favorite part of the visit. We had gone up to Taos overnight on Tuesday and Wednesday. Ves wanted to visit her old friend Philip who lives there with his wife and baby Lucia. We met him just at sunset and had a great walk in the snow along the rim of the Rio Grande gorge which is an incredible thing. Ves said Es was really looking forward to seeing a big canyon and did she ever! Es had a huge shy attack, just dying of embarrassment, when she was introduced to Philip - turned out she thought he was Prince Philip from Sleeping Beauty. Philip directed us to a funky good restaurant for dinner, Apple Love, and we had a fine time there. We stayed overnight at the Sagebrush Inn and had a fire in the kiva fireplace and got all snuggly. The next day was a beautiful sunny winter day. We wandered around on the streets behind the plaza and came upon this fabulous toy store with a very creative play ground in the back. The whole place was so whimsical, it looked like it had been built by fairies. The lady in the toy store told us that a song circle was starting up in ten minutes upstairs, it was free, and we were welcome to join. It was a half dozen young moms and dads with their pre-school age kids. There was singing, dancing, and instrument playing led by a perky young mom who had moved to Taos from Wisconsin. I think Es enjoyed it although she's not much of a joiner-inner. Afterward she ran all over the incredible playground and did everything twice. We hung out a while at the Moby Dickens bookstore and then walked out to the Mabel Dodge Luhan estate on the outskirts. We didn't know if we could get in or not or what was going on there, it wasn't marked on the town map. But not only did we get in, the docent invited us to have some coffee and cookies while we looked around. It's a conference center now. I've read all about this house and Mabel Dodge and Tony Luhan and all the famous artists and writers she hosted so this was a real treat for me. We had a very scary experience driving up to Taos. There's a seven mile stretch between Espanola and Taos with overhanging cliffs and signs alongside the road showing a car graphic with rocks falling down. I've never given it much thought before but that day we saw a boulder the size of a refrigerator bounce down the hill and fly across the road right in front of us, bounce once more and fly into the river. It must have been going 60 miles an hour. If it had hit us we would all have died instantly. We were so freaked I can't tell you. It's like you can't believe your eyes. Someone at the library told me that about 15 years ago a big boulder like that fell on a school bus and all the kids were killed. Other than that, the visit was really really fun. We did stuff every day like the dinosaur museum, visited my library in Placitas and got NM kid books, went for hikes in the arroyos around here. Es loves to climb so we went on the steep hills around here with both the cats along as well as Ves and Silvi in her pouch. Dave and Silvi really hit it off - every time I looked he was carrying the baby around or sitting with her on his lap. She's a happy, easygoing baby, always smiling, cooing and gurgling like she's trying to talk. Essie was a riot, busy busy busy into everything. She says the most startling things sometimes, like the other night we all sat down to dinner and Ves was still on the phone. Essie says "mama needs to join us at the table." One night she sat on my lap and watched part of "V." Es was thrilled to be watching a scary show – I covered her eyes a few times. Then a few days later she whispers to me with round eyes, "Did you see the tail coming out of the baby's diaper?" We watched Toy Story 3 about three times and Es who was totally riveted watching the movie, out of the blue suddenly vomited, poor girl. This happened two nights in a row. Mysterious and disturbing. Ves is worried that it's connected to her seizures. Both times, she said she felt fine afterward, but she was ready to go to bed.

She had a lot of fun with the cats, running around the house with them, romping and carrying on. Junie was right in there every minute playing the silly buggers. We had to drag him off their bed at night and put him out of the room so they could sleep. He's really a good family cat. Now he's moping around like he's depressed. I say "do you miss Essie, June?" and he gives me a forlorn look. I miss Es too! She has such a sense of humor. She was peeling an orange and struggling with the end bit. I said "pull out that belly button Es !" She looked surprised and then just fell apart laughing. And she kept coming back to it later and repeating what I said and laughing and laughing.

So the sad day came on Friday and we took them to the airport. We helped Ves get the suitcase and car seats up to the curbside check in. Dave had to walk away to the curb to deal with a cop who had pulled up by our car and wanted us to move on. Es saw him leaving and said "I have to say good-bye to Dave" and ran across the sidewalk to give him a hug. He was really touched because he thought Es didn't like him, even though Ves and I kept telling him she was just acting like a three-year-old, 'the new two' with all her no no no no no no and refusal to sit in his lap or hold his hand. She's a girl who knows exactly what she wants and doesn't want and Ves is the sweetest, nicest Mom a kid could want. I'm really proud of her !!

Wednesday, March 23, 2011

Arrived at the airport at dusk and was picked up by the whole family. Everyone was happy to see me. Joyous time. At home Es wanted to see what I had brought her so I pulled out the presents, mostly papers, tape, stickers etc. and an outfit for Es and one for Silvi, two camisoles for Ves which alas were a bit too large. Ves said that Es wanted me to sleep with her which I was all too happy to do, a dream fulfilled actually, so Es and I slept together for the next week. She's a great snuggler and a heavy sleeper, dreams all night it seems with great breathing and deep silences, grinding of teeth and laughing. I would wake up a few times during the night to find myself on the very edge of the mattress so I would wake a little and move Es over to her side then have to jump back in quickly before she reclaimed the territory. She sleeps in just her underpants so I would sometimes wake up aware that she was uncovered and cold. She would murmur 'please cover me up' which I did. The first night we stayed up for a long time talking and laughing. Ves and Jer said they could hear us from their room and were silently howling with laughter, esp. about the 'noonoo'piñata.'. Es is into piñatas these days and when we were talking about what kind of piñata she would like best, she suggested a 'noonoo' piñata. I didn't get it at the time but found out later that 'noonoo' is Es' nickname for Silvi (newnew). Es treated me to her bathroom humor and great sense of comic timing. She would say, with a droll deadpan look on her face, "it's a …..dramatic pause….. POOP! followed by gales of laughter. She did this over and over and I laughed every time time too. Her timing was really good. If Ves and Jer heard her, they would say "that's really not very nice Essie" which of course only encouraged her.

Silvi is totally adorable. I would find her 'studying' me with a grave serious look and then when she knew I knew she was watching me, she would break out into a beautiful smile, head cocked to one side. Totally heartbreaking. She's quickly moving through crawling to standing, holding on with one hand and moving one foot up and down ready to take off walking. Sandy said that Jer walked at 8 months and I think Silvi will be there too. She's really trying hard to talk too, making these funny purring sounds and vocalizing with her throat. She watches every move that Essie makes and is thrilled when Es plays with her, NooNoo grabbing at her hair and beaming. Es definitely has mixed emotions about her new baby sister. This is a great character builder, I think, and I'm sure that Ves and Jer will have the finesse and sensitivity to guide her through it. Es asked me a lot of questions about my little sister which

I was happy to answer. Then she asked me if my sister is "as silly" as I am. I said yes…, taking this as a compliment. I did a lot of 'talking' the dolls and animals. One hilarious time I was 'talking' Emily the doll and Es was pressing me for more so Emily said "I would like to talk about my feelings.' Es was immediately on the wavelength. I/Emily told her of how the stuffed animals didn't like me because they had this beautiful fur and all I had was this ugly underwear. She was totally empathetic and told me (Emily) in a very roundabout diplomatic way that I was a very nice girl but "Emily I have to say this, you're ….ugly." At that point, Emily cried, and Es leaped off the bed to rummage through her dress-up playclothes and came up with a glamorous outfit for Emily. She dressed her up in a sparkly blue dress and a necklace, then we all promptly went to sleep.

So I spent the days hanging out with the girls, picking Es up at Promise Preschool with Silvi along in the stroller. This was Silvi's first experience with the stroller and I can say confidently that she LOVED it. Es would ride up front on the prow. When we got to a cross street, Es would jump off and ran around to hold hands with me to cross the street. It worked out fine. Ves put on a birthday party for me on Saturday night that was fun. We did delicious brats from the Old World meat store, sauteed red cabbage and apple, and Sandy brought hot potato salad that was great. Ves made me a German Chocolate cake that was wonderful. The party included Vince and Sandy and Vincene and David who were visiting from Austin. I hadn't seen them since the wedding. Then Sandy invited me to her house for scones (sour cherry, the best ever) and coffee the Tuesday I had Silvi for the morning. We had a very cheerful time visiting and NooNoo was happy too. Sandy has an old fashioned wooden high chair that she bought at a flea market that she has to tie Silvi in with a big napkin around her tummy. Silvi is perfectly comfortable and happy at Ama's house which was a big relief to me as

NooNoo is at that age when she is figuring out who are her people and who are not. She pretty much accepted me most of the time but there were times when she would yell and yell and I mean really loud until her eyebrows were red and she was sobbing uncontrollably. She could do this from zero to sixty in two minutes. Next time I see her, of course, that will be all over and she'll be into a new phase....probably running all over the yard on her own two feet !! On my last night there, we went to the Scenic for dinner and that was a real treat. The girls behaved perfectly and Esme loved her kid dinner – tater tots and grilled cheese and fruit. She said "they know what kids like" I'll be back in late June for Essie's birthday – can't wait !!

July 1, 2011

Duluth was cool and green, lilacs blooming everywhere. I was there for Esme's 4th birthday party that she said would be "the best party of my life." It was a hot, sunny day after many days of cool, rainy weather. Jer set up a shade tent and Ves decorated it with streamers and balloons. The worm piñata that Dave sent was a hit although none of the kids could break it. Finally a Mom stepped up and gave it a good whack and all the goodies fell out for the kids to collect in the little tin buckets Ves bought as party favors. The worm was full of insect finger puppets, bird whistles and good fruit candy. The twins Edward and Isaac were there with their harried looking mom. I've heard so much about these boys; it was nice to meet them. They are a year older than the girls and were intent on exploring the house but Jer headed them off at every turn. Brandy came late with her twins Dot and Lot who are getting prettier every year. The little girls, about six of them, all dressed up in Essie's play dress-up outfits and everyone enjoyed the carrot cake cupcakes that Es helped me decorate with green 'fairy dust' (sprinkles) and Johnny jump ups from the lawn. Es has been deep into fairy stuff after watching the lastest kid movie "Tinkerbell" on dvd. I watched it twice with her and must say I enjoyed it both times. Nu (Sylvi) is really precious. She's only 10 months old but she's already taking steps and saying 'dad' and 'daddy' and to my surprise 'Ba' once. She watches every move her sister makes and tries to join in. She's at that stage where she won't let her mama out of her sight. As soon as Ves leaves the room she starts crying and she is loud and inconsolable. Within a minute or two, her eyebrows are red and she's sodden with tears. Then moments later when mama is restored, she'll flash out the most brilliant smile and fling out her arm to you in greeting

We went up to Ely for the weekend and met up with Jer who was attempting (unsuccessfully) to bicycle there from Duluth (it was too swampy on the trails he took). We stayed in their friend Lara's cute little cabin and went to the town lake all day Saturday and swam and canoed. Es loves the water and has learned some good moves at her winter swimming classes. Some bigger kids came to the beach with huge alligator and killer whale floats that Es was dying to get on but they turned ignored her pleas – it was sad to see. Her dad appropriated a noodle from their pile of beach toys and Es played happily on that until Jer returned it. On our next trip to Cub, we got Es her own noodle. We had two fine dinners at the Chocolate Moose and on the way home on Sunday stopped at a carnival and Es and her mom and dad went on the rides. I think her favorite was one teeny rollercoaster that she went on with two other girls.

It was a good visit. Essie and I played a lot of shopping. She has what Ves calls "Essie Style" – no one dresses Es anymore but Es and her outfits are very creative. We slept together every night in her bed which is delightful – however – she's beginning to complain about my snoring......

I'll see them all again the end of this month when Dave and I drive up to Minnesota with our camper. We plan to arrive on July 28 and will camp out in their back alley and take a few camping trips during the week, leaving August 15.

August 21, 2011

'bout time I wrote about our truly wonderful epic three weeks + vacation camping with the kids. We left on July 21 and drove up to Lake McConnaughey, Nebraska to spend our first night on its sandy shores. Dave had been there before and raved about how pretty it was, how warm the water, how sandy the beach. It turned out to be awful. As we learned, all the rivers and lakes in the Midwest were still at or above flood stage and Lake McConnaughey was no exception. There was no shoreline to speak of, it was crowded and smelled bad. We threw up our camper with the last bit of light. Then the industrial strength generator of the RV next to us came on, a huge wind started blowing, showering grit on us all night, and when dawn arrived we got up and hurriedly threw it all together and drove away, who knew where, we just wanted to get the hell out of there. I remember whining to Dave "maybe we should just go home….." We decided to drive north up through the backroads of Nebraska to a big open space on the map called the Sand Hills. We saw on the map a largish lake in the upper corner of this mysterious country and headed for it. What a surprise to discover a beautiful open country of lush rolling green hills. The lake was Merritt Reservoir State Park, very nicely kept and we found a private sandy beach all to ourselves. There were very few people there. We stayed three days and the longer we stayed the more we felt this was a magical place, so clean and natural, just something special and sparkly about it. The lake was full of big fish, muskies, northerns, bass, walleyes, croppies but very few people and it just had that wild feeling that Jackson Hole used to have. On Monday we left, and stopped in at the only small town in the whole area, Valentine, and had breakfast. Valentine is at the confluence of the Snake and Niobrara rivers and is a river kayaking, canoeing and tubing center. We want to go back. I'd love to bicycle through the McKelvie National Forest, all grasslands with a paved bike path through it, located right next to Merritt. We spent the day driving across Nebraska into Minnesota and arrived at Peter & Judy's house in Owatonna around sunset on Monday, August 25. We spent the next three days with Peter, Judy and Ruby, their boxer, a very sweet big dog. Dave and I just love Peter and Judy – we talked and talked, ate and drank, played croquet which was really fun, went for a walk in one of Owatonna's many nice parks, and talked and talked some more. Dave and I marveled at how humid, green and buggy it was – but beautiful.

On Thursday, August 28, we drove up to Duluth and arrived just before dinnertime. Ves and Jer's next door neighbor, agreed to let us use his asphalt parking area behind the alley and next to Essie's 'Firewoods' a small patch of jungly woods. We stayed there for three nights and it was good to have our own space and yet be able to hang out in Ves and Jer's house too. We had nice dinners and time with the kids and Ves. Es slept with me every night, so cute, she came out to the camper with her jeweled bag, stuffed animal, books, nightgown or jammies and her camplight. We would do our nighttime routine, she would pretend to floss, we would brush teeth, have a cheerios snack and read a few books before falling asleep, making sure the 'cold water' was within reach. Es resists falling asleep but when she does, she is out for the next 10-11 hours solid, not even thunder and lightning will wake her up, as we found out camping in Herbster, Wisconsin, where we went for our first camping trip. Ves and the girls, Dave and I caravanned on Sunday to this spot that is only an hour or so away from Duluth but it seemed like a world apart. Herbster is a tiny town on the south shore of Lake Superior adjacent to the Apostle Islands. The camp ground was a grassy field next to a woods and right on the shore. We had a sandy beach to play on and a nice kids' playground. The weather was hot and sunny with the exception of a very stormy and rainy night on Tuesday. Vince, Sandy and Jer came on Monday to stay overnight and leave around noon on Tuesday so Jer could get to work. We all had a wonderful breakfast before they left featuring biscuits made by Jer in the Dutch oven along with bacon and scrambled eggs, good strong coffee. Dave and I enjoy Vince and Sandy so much.

On Thursday, we drove back to Duluth, stopping at an authentic fifties diner for brunch on the way and back at the house, set up again in Bill's parking lot. The next night was movie night in the park. What a delightful time – we joined a couple hundred other people with their kids to watch "Finding Nemo." It was Essie's first big screen movie and she was riveted. That weekend, Dave kept intercepting Nu climbing the stairs then turning around and teetering at the top of the stairs since she didn't know how to climb down so he taught her how to turn around on her belly and climb down safely. She's a very bright baby and picked it right up and further applied it to getting down off the bed and the sofa.

On Sunday, we took off again, this time to McCarthy Beach State Park a few hours from Duluth to the northwest. This was quite a different camping experience from Herbster. And best of all for Dave, free hot showers ! Rather than a grassy open field we were in a deep, dark woods, a peninsula running between two lakes: Side Lake and Sturgeon Lake. Our camp was right on Side Lake with a little dock onto the water. Clear warm water with a sandy bottom. Jer brought his canoe along and everyone went out for a paddle throughout the three days that Jer and his parents were there. I went out with Ves and Jer for a long paddle. Jer fished from the canoe – he hooked a big one once but it got away. The woods were pretty, huge old white and red pines interspersed with birch and aspen – 'fairy woods' Essie called them, and we hiked the lakeside trail several times. The story was that townspeople back in the 40s raised the money to buy the land from the timber company in order to preserve some of the last remaining old white pines in the area and the state park was created. We would bicycle or walk over to Sturgeon every day to swim at the bathing beach that had nice changing rooms, picnic tables and benches, shallow water that went out a long way and a big sandy beach – perfect sand for making sculptures according to Avesa. She made a wonderful elephant. I wondered how she was going to do the body and she cleverly put him on his knees with trunk up as though he were swimming. Some punk kid wrecked it before the day was out.....Es had her new bike with training wheels along – the park was perfect for biking. Little kids bombed around the paths and Es soberly witnessed many a wipeout. I think it was good for her to see that....she made some good progress on her bike riding that week – and swimming. It was Nu's birthday on the 11th and we had a little party with cupcake for her while her dad, PopPop and Ama were there (they had to leave after three days again so Jer could get to work). We all sang Happy Birthday to her and she got all shy and looked down, ducking her head to the side – cute ! Ama presented a wonderful album of Sylvi's first year in photos.

So it was back to Ves and Jer's house for an overnight stay, then down to Peter and Judy's for an overnight there and then the long ride home. We stayed one night at Johnson Lake near Sandy's old hometown of Gothenburg, Neb. then drove a long long day home down the eastern side of Colorado to Trinidad and on to home. Everything was fine back at the house and the kitties were very glad to see us again.

November 11, 2011

This time I visited for Halloween, Essie's favorite holiday. Duluth was very pleasant weather-wise, just a little chilly and plenty of color left on the trees. Sandy picked me up with the girls and we went back to Ves and Jer's house. First on the agenda was opening the suitcase and going through all the presents. Es loved her 'sparkly shoes' and Nu is too little to care about any of it. Then Es wanted to go upstairs right away and play shopping (that was Sandy's chance to split – they were worried that Nu would be scared with me – she wasn't a bit) I was happy to see that Es is being very nice to her sister now, letting her join in and treating her very tenderly. How could anyone resist the charms of Sylvia aka Nu? She's just the happiest, jolliest little girl and smart as a whip. She lights up when her big sister says "come play with me, Nu." It made me very happy to see this change. Once again, I slept with Es every night and it was delightful. Poor girl has some anxiety going in her sleep, grinding her molars and whimpering with bad dreams. This is the lot of the oldest child, I think. If I was awake when this was going on, I would rub her back until she relaxed back into deeper sleep. We had a lot of fun playing shopping, dress up and fort building. On Wednesday and Monday, I was in charge of waking them up, getting them dressed, fed and out the door to be on time for Essie's preschool at 9:00. We had to get up in the dark at 7:15 to accomplish this; Ves had already left for work. Es woke up right away because she loves school but then the argument was on about what to wear. I understand this is a daily battle. Essie woke Nu up very gently and she woke up with a big smile. We made it on time both days, rolling down the hill in the stroller and back up again, only to repeat in two hours when we picked Es up. Good exercise and an opportunity to stop in at the supermarket to pick up things for dinner, then home for lunch and play. Then – the big day arrived – Halloween. Since it was on Monday, I got Es up and she dressed in her ballet costume with the fairy ring crown. She looked beautiful. I tried to get her hair up in a proper ballet bun but didn't do so hot a job on it. Her hair is very slippery, hard to get up. She had fun at school – her friend Imogene was there that day after having been sick the previous week. As I rolled out of the preschool lobby I could see all the kids galloping in a circle like mad. When Ves and Jer came home, I made pastitsio for dinner – Vince and Sandy came over – Nu gave the most amazing crow of delight when she saw Vince get out of the car. We had a quick dinner before we went out. Ves had the witches' cauldron full of candy by the door and every piece went before the evening was out. Jer lit the pumpkins they carved on the weekend. The front porch was decorated with all kinds of drawings and decorations that Ves made with the girls. Es changed into her second costume – the bee – and Nu dressed as a witch in Es' costume from last year. We went out to trick or treat and met up with Ves and Jer's new neighbors and their kids. Vince stayed behind to give out candy. We were out about an hour – Essie had quite a haul in her bucket – which she sorted out on the floor and got into an argument with her mother about where to store it. She says indignantly to Ves, "You don't know ANYTHING about candy !" After Vince and Sandy left, we got in the car and went to a haunted house that was really scary – very elaborate, something this guy does every year. It was mobbed and full of screaming teenage girls. Es wanted to go in – sort of – but her mom and dad thought it would be too much. Ves and I went through the 'tunnel' and it was frightening for us. I left the next day. We stopped for lunch at Culvers which Essie loves. We all shared the wonderful strawberry shake. It was a great visit, I'm so glad I got to spend Halloween with those sweet girls. Will see them again in early January.

January 29, 2012

The visit from Ves, Jer and the girls has come and gone and it was a wonderful time. They arrived on Wed. afternoon, we had an early posole dinner then set out on a walk to the top of one of the cerros I can see from this window. We got there at sunset and the light was magical. We did the Christmas stockings and gift exchange when we got home. The next day Jer took the train up to Santa Fe where he had a bike rental arranged at Mellow Velo – he had quite an adventure and returned home delighted. Ves, Es, Silvi and I went to the library and to the playground at the church in the village then home to play with the cats. Junie and Will were so good with the girls, I think they really enjoyed one another. Ves says I don't need to have any toys when they come, the cats are enough. We played a lot of 'cat and coyote' games, much of it in the car in the driveway. I pulled down the seat in the back and Es could crawl in to the 'coyote den.' They really enjoyed playing in the stereo closet too. Silvi loved pulling out the cassettes and putting them back in different slots. I had a wonderful moment with her when I was changing her diaper. She looked intently at me then pointed and said "Baba." She said Baba a lot after that…..she's such an adorable girl, full of joy. She's Essie's quiet little sidekick, always there, watching and joining in very tactfully. Essie has her well trained – Es is very sweet to her but if Nu makes a bad move, Es cuts in with a sharp 'No' and Nu instantly minds her. Now and then, though, Nu will rear up and lash back and Es backs off with 'okay, okay.' I got to spend a lot of time with them alone which was so great. We played pretend nonstop. The girls liked playing with the pretty rocks in the garden out front too. We also did 'dance parties' with Ves and Sil is quite the dancer. Ves and Jer took advantage of the grandparents to go off to the Jemez and hike through the snow to a hot springs and also to a movie another day, things they never get to do at home, they say. We all went together to the Indian dances on January 6 to Santo Domingo. We met up with Alana and her friend Tenaya and watched the dances then got invited to lunch at the lt. governor's house. It was nice – hot chile, turkey and stuffing, fruit cups and when we left, one of the ladies gave us two big bags of bread. Es really liked the bread and asked for pieces of 'Indian bread buttered please' many times in the next days. After the lunch we drove over to Cochiti Pueblo to see their dances but they were closed to the public so we left and went to Tent Rocks for a hike. It was a gorgeous day and the hike through the slot canyon was amazing. Pretty snowy and slippery but we made it. Jer took loads of pictures. The next day, another gorgeous day, we went to Santa Fe and walked around Canyon Road and had lunch at the Compound. That night we watched "The Black Stallion" The whole day was a treat. Before we knew it though, it was Tuesday, and time to leave. We went to the Biopark and did a quick tour of the aquarium and the park, then a quick lunch at Lotaburger where Silvi had her first French fry dipped in ketchup the same place where Essie had her first burger and fries and then off to the airport. What a great time we had !

Thursday, April 5, 2012

Got back on Tuesday from visiting the girls in Duluth. Essie is now 4 ½ and Nu is 18 months. Just as cute and lively as can be. I brought them Easter candy and toys, sparkly headbands and Skechers for Es, too big for now, unfortunately. Also two story books about Tibet from Aunt Alana, one of which was a big hit with the scary but thrilling yeti stories. We never did get to read the second book, Es was so deep into the first one she wasn't ready to move on to the second. I like that about her, she feels deeply, she wants to savor. The next morning I took both Es and Nu down to Promise at 9:00. Es loves her school. While I was there we visited one of her options for kindergarten which was a rundown old school building in the poor part of town. Sounds bad but we were all impressed by the principal and also by the tour given by a personable fifth grade boy. I liked the music room which had a rich funky vibe – lots of instruments and African drums and an atmosphere of calm but vibrant energy. Ves loved the multicultural mix, just like San Francisco she said. The downside is that it is a poor neighborhood with all the attendant ills that Es would have to deal with, and she is a sensitive girl, so who knows how she would experience the school. Could go a lot of ways, but Ves and Jer are concerned and rightfully so. On the next trip down to Promise to pick up Es, Sil stayed behind with Jer so Es and I stopped in at Walgreens on the way home and I bought her a big stuffed pink Easter bunny and a pink Easter bonnet– she loved them. I told Es that she had to share the bunny with Nu and she did a pretty good job of it although the bunny was undoubtedly belonging to Es. Ves let me know that I need to start buying stuff for Nu just like Es and I agree. Up til now, Sil was too young to notice but she does now. She is a dear girl. She was kind of shy of me at first but was getting used to me by the time I left. On the last night there, Ves and Es went to the swim lesson at the Y leaving me and Nu at home alone. Nu woke up from her nap and at first gave me a happy smile which quickly turned into loud yelling and crying when she discovered her mom and dad were not home. She soon recovered, red-faced and sobbing and sat on my lap to eat a bowl of cheddar rabbit crackers. It was so cute, she would eat one cracker and then offer the next one to me, putting it in my mouth, heaving sobs all the while. She's a spirited dancer, twirling and swirling and galloping like a horse. She has the most beautiful little hands with tapered fingers, the hands of an artist, and she hates messy fingers, always wiping her hands with a napkin at the table. She and Es get along fine; Es is very tender towards her most of the time, calls her 'little one.' They play nicely together. Nu loves the dollhouse Marv gave them. Essie and I played a lot of pretend but no 'shopping' this time.

Ves and Jer took us all to dinner at a nice restaurant for my birthday present and Es presented me with the most wonderful drawing of the two of us as her present. It is truly remarkable – I'm going to frame it. Right now it's on the fridge where I can look at it a lot. It will be so nice to see the girls again in summer for long camping trips. This time of year in Duluth was gloomy and we didn't get to play outside much. I made some dinners that Ves and Jer liked a lot like my weekday version of jambalaya with chicken, sausage, peppers and stewed tomatoes, also a stir fry with leftover steak that Ves thought was mighty tasty but the girls were unimpressed and often ended up with a peanut butter sandwich for dinner. Essie likes blueberries, bread and butter the most. We do share a love of parmesan goldfish.

July 9 to August 10, 2012

Back from the big trip – we were gone a month, a record for us camping in the pop-up. The first day we made it to the Lake Mac on the Platte. The sandy beaches were back, it reminded me of Elephant Butte. We stayed two nights and were on our way to the Sand Hills and Merritt Lake. Big disappointment, the lush green hills were brown and the lake was full of green algae. We fled to the Samuel R. McKelvie National Forest nearby and stayed a night at Steer Creek Campground, all dried up, lots of lowing steers all night. This is an artificial forest, a small patch of pines in a sea of rolling hills of grass. We were the only campers there. It was HOT and the pines were sizzling. It turned out to be a very pleasant spot to camp overnight though, kinda of a ghostly campground full of strange sounds and smells. Dave and I went for a bike ride all around the campground and up the highway at dusk. We found an unoccupied ranger compound of several houses and barns and were able to get some clean water from their pump. I wonder where they all were…. It looked like they just left. It finally got cool around 5 a.m

On Sunday, July 29, Ves drove down to the Cities to pick up Jen, her new boyfriend Ted, and Danny. They all left on a wilderness canoe trip to Quetico the next day, leaving Dave and me in charge of Es and Nuie for the week. Ves' biggest worry was that we wouldn't get any sleep with Nu waking up at 5 am crying as she has been doing. This did happen the first night and I got in bed with them and quieted her down in about 40 minutes. The next morning we had a talk, I told Es and Nu that their parents had called to say hello, they were having fun with their friends on a canoe trip and they would be home in a week, not to worry. Sil was sitting on my lap as I said this and I could literally feel her body relax. She slept through the night for the rest of the week. I think she just needed to know what's going on and she can understand a LOT. It was so cute – once I looked in at 8:30 to see if they were up yet and there was Nu snuggled up next to her sleeping sister, big smile. She waved hello to me and as I walked into the room she waved me away as if to say 'leave us alone' so I did. When I looked in a little later, they were both up with books open on their pillows, side by side kneeling up in bed reading, totally absorbed. The girls are adorable the way they snuggle together in bed. One night at bedtime, Silvers was feeling sad and she said "Way Way" (her name for Es) in the most plaintive little voice, it was heartbreaking. Es immediately took her in her arms and they snuggled off to sleep in minutes. The weather was beautiful all that week and we went to the beach every single day, either to sandy Park Point or to rocky Brighton Beach. The lake water was warm and clear, just gorgeous. Essie and I spent HOURS in the water swimming. She worked really hard at her swimming and made good progress. She used her face mask to dive down and pick things up off the bottom. Usually, Nubers would fall asleep in the truck driving to the beach so Dave would take the car seat out and carry her to a spot in the shade to finish her nap. One day, we were playing a Sade cd and I could hear crooning from the back seat and turned to look – there's Silvi with her lips pursed up singing "bluuuu…." By the end of the week, after watching her sister swim she wanted to do the same – she copies EVERYTHING her sister does – so Dave and I would push her back and forth between us in the watr and she would kick her legs and 'swim'. She was very proud of herself. I would usually pack a lunch and try to keep the 'racoons' out of the cooler, but we had many a sandy sandwich. Sometimes we had fast food like KFC, Culvers or Wendy's and the girls loved that. We grilled steaks and chops (the kitchen was SO hot to cook in) and Es surprised me with what a carnivore she is – she cleaned out the bones and ate all her meat and some of ours too. One night we went to Ama and PopPop's for dinner. Dave thought he knew the way there but when we got to the top of the hill, he was lost. Essie said she knew the way and directed Dave right to their house, even at one point, we both said, "no, that can't be right" but it was. Dave was amazed and went on and on about it. Es was chuffed.

I worked hard at keeping the girls from getting sunburnt and succeeded with constant sunblock buttering. It was very hard work to take care of them all week, make no bones about it. There were a few bad picnic table tumbles, a bee sting and a few other other scrapes but nothing worse thank god. When we got up every morning, it was diaper change, dress, breakfast, num nums (vitamins) hair brushing, tooth brushing, then play for a little while then get ready for the beach which meant slathering with sunblock, finding shoes and swimsuits, packing lunch then out the door. Then at the door often there was only one shoe to be found or they would come to the door looking like Maoris covered in magic marker drawings all over their bodies. It washed right off, but then more sunblock was needed and where oh where is that other flippy? I admit I lost it a few times howling Stop Stop Stop. The girls were instantly sobered when I did that and were more than willing to comply with whatever I wanted which was good but I did feel bad about losing control like that. They didn't seem to hold it against me at all. All in all we had a really good time. One day we went to the aquarium which Es was crazy about and another day we went to the new Children's Museum in West Duluth. We ended up staying there all afternoon until closing and the girls had a ball, they were off and running as soon as we got there. All the medieval castle playthings from the old children's museum were there along with a lot of new things. They were doing face painting that day and Dave painted both Es and Nu to their delight – he painted Es as a 'skeleton butterfly'. Es played with some girls all afternoon. It was funny – Sil was napping in the truck so I sat with her and when she woke up we went into the museum. She saw Es and walked up to her then realized she was playing with girls her own age. She immediately turned and walked away to do something else. Such tact ! It was great to get to know Silvi better during this week. I love the way she goes "mmhmmm" for 'yes' and "unhunh" for 'no.' We got very close during the week, she was even calling me 'mama' and coming to me for comfort – she would realize she had called me mama and correct herself and say baba. Es and I got closer too and had some good talks in bed going to sleep. One night, she talked about Santa Claus and confided in me that she's not sure he's for real. I did not confirm or deny. Essie is growing up – when she went to the bathroom, she would shut the door and say she "wanted some privacy" but then she would shout for me to come and "wipe my bottom." We talked a lot about kindergarten coming up and read a book every night about a kid's first day at kindergarten – she's got some trepidations. She's worried about it being all day; I don't blame her but I reassured her about how much fun it would be.

We were on the beach at Park Point the day Ves and Jer returned. The girls seemed stunned at first to see them then terribly excited. Nu would not even look at me after that – Dave said I was 'sugar on the floor.' So true, but I didn't take it personally. We had a little birthday celebration for Nuie the next night, cupcakes – she blew out the candles – twice – and she opened the presents I brought: an outfit and three board books that she liked. I'll see them again in October !

Dave helped Ves clean the house the next day and Jer played with the girls. I just took it easy on the porch. I had done all the work of taking care of the girls so I felt I deserved a break. Ves and Jer were scandalized that Dave refused to change a diaper – I didn't care though. Ves treated us to a nice steak dinner that night, we had Nu's party and we left the next morning. Stopped overnight at Peter and Judy's which is always fun - they're so happy about their new granddaughter Gretchen - then took off the next morning for the long drive home. We spent the night at Ft. Kearney State Park along the Platte in Nebraska, a very nice stopover and then a long day's drive home arriving at midnight. We listened to a Mario Puzo audio book 'Omerta' –pretty good.

November 8, 2012

Visited the girls for a week over Halloween and had a great time... mostly getting to know our Nu.....who is "me no baby" now at 26 months. For most of my visit, Ves and Essie would leave the house at 7:15 to go off to their schools (Es is now at all day kindergarten). Jer was working days. At first, I had a brief panic as in 'what am I going to do with a two-year old all day?' but my fears were unfounded. Sil and I moved smoothly through the day and had a very good time together. She's putting together two and three word sentences. I'm sure next time I see her she will be speaking in complete sentences. She has a great sense of humor – both girls do. We went to Super One to buy some stuff one day and I spotted a plastic-wrapped package of fish heads, big eyes and sharp pointy noses, local fish – smelts?. I said to Nu "look, here's lunch for us!" She burst out laughing, totally got the joke. I showed her some cute animal things on the internet that she wanted to see over and over again, ""Gen Baba, 'gen." Hillary sent me an emailed Halloween card that was like a little movie and we must've watched that 15 times.

Ves has a very nice dinner time custom going wherein we all hold hands before diving in and say what we are grateful for. Nu always said "Ama's house.' I made some really good dinners that I know Jer for one really enjoyed, the girls not so much. Es was all excited about the spaghetti and meatballs dinner but was visibly deflated when she saw the meat sauce on top of the spaghetti…Ves said "oh, no, you didn't put the sauce on top, did you?" Jeez…I didn't know.

Essie has grown up a lot since the summer – kindergarten is good for her. She's speaking well, no temper tantrums, just all around more mature and a delightful, happy girl with that droll sense of humor. Ves and the girl carved Halloween pumpkins, lots of creative variety. One had a sort of twisted grin with blocky teeth. I told Es his name was Chucky. We both thought that was hilarious and she brought it up again a few times, saying "Chucky" in her fake deep gravelly voice then laughing all over again.

I don't get to sleep with Es anymore since she and Nu are sleeping together which is SO cute. I slept on Ama's blow up bed in the living room – the girls had a great time bouncing on it for hours. Es and Silvi have a sweet relationship…most of the time. One day we were out shopping at the mall. Ves and Jer ran into a store and left me with the girls in the car. I looked around at them in their car seats and Nu took Essie's hand in hers, kind of clumsily and said fervently "My WayWay" (her name for Esme). Es didn't say anything but I think she was touched. Ves told me that Es had told her earlier that she didn't know if Sil loved her or not. I think she showed her with that!

I'll see them again at Christmas – this year, they're coming here !

January 10, 2013

Christmas has come and gone. We had a fine time. They got in Christmas Eve afternoon, came back to the house – the girls liked the room I fixed up for them with lots of pillows and sheets for forts, toys and a 'writing center' as Essie called it. But they didn't care for the cardboard box tunnel which surprised me. After a cursory examination, they never went in it again. We had posole which Ves swooned over – it was Dave's best batch ever I think. Then we drove up to Santa Fe to do the Canyon Road walk which turned out to be grueling and no fun really. That event is too crowded now, parking is a nightmare, very few farolitos, no galleries open, no singing and crowds and crowds of people. I wanted to go to Jemez Pueblo the next day, Christmas Day, but everyone was too pooped from the SF excursion the night before. We had a nice breakfast and opened presents. Santa left the girls a nice note about how he was able to find them. Essie was pretty impressed with that but she's skeptical and is noting the discrepancies. She loved loved loved the Barbie Fashionista and the princess backpack complete with high heel shoes. Nu was literally stunned when she opened her present of the Rapunzel doll. Later, we had a prime rib dinner that was pretty disastrous due to the new grill. On Boxing Day, Jer left the house at 4:00 a.m. to drive down to Bosque del Apache to shoot the birds – he took 400 pictures. We drove down to arrive at noon with a picnic lunch and hiked and drove around the refuge for the afternoon culminating in the sundown return of the birds, clouds of cranes and snow geese. It was quite a scene with the German and Japanese birders and their $40,000 cameras. Jer loved it, Essie said "birds are boring" although she thought the possibility of getting attacked by a mountain lion was pretty exciting. There were warning signs everywhere. We stopped in Los Lunas on the way home to have dinner at Andra's house. She gave Ves bags and bags of beautiful clothing for the girls, really overwhelming. The next day, Ves and Jer took the train to Santa Fe to stay overnight at a hotel. They said they had a wonderful time, Jer took gorgeous pictures and they got to enjoy breakfast at one of my faves, the Swiss Bakery. We had the girls overnight – I made pancakes for dinner at their request and we watched a great dvd about a horse "Spirit...." Nuie started to cry a few times missing her mama but we were able to comfort her. Es did a great job of that, bringing her so many stuffed animals that Nu started to laugh. Nu was so sweet and trusting with me. In the morning, she came out plaintively calling "mommy, mommy?" I told her they were on a little trip and I would be her mama for the day. She said "otay" and went happily off to play. Later, she came up to me and held up her arms saying "Baba, I need you." She just wanted to be picked up and hugged. I've seen her do that with her parents and I felt so honored she would ask me ! She is a dear girl. We took them to the Natural History Museum to look at the fossils and have lunch later at Blakes and a nice drive home down Rio Grande and Rt 66. At home, Es and I set off with a basket to search for fossils. Essie likes it here. She told me she really likes that you can see all the way out to the "edges." On Saturday, we went to a Kwanzaa party that was quite an ordeal. Ves and Jer slipped away to go home and eat. Jer had run to the top of the Sandias that afternoon and was starved out. Dave and I stayed and endured endless testimony about the principle of economic cooperation. Never again. Es played with two girls who got in trouble playing with printers ink in the bathroom. Es didn't have any paint on her fingers though so she was innocent of wrongdoing. We went home as soon as we could and watched "The Marigold Hotel" and ate cookies so it turned out a fun evening after all. Sunday, their last day, we went down to the Tamaya and hiked around in their bosque. It was an iron gray cold day though. We went home to relax and put together the roast beef burrito dinner. Andra came and we had a very nice dinner with all the crystal and silver on the table. Dave was dying to do that and we did. They were up early the next morning greeted by a snowstorm. I was going to take them to the airport but I asked Dave to and he returned saying it was pretty hairy, lots of wrecks. But they got off okay and Ves called later to say all was well. Sigh....I'll see them again in March, I hope.

April 22 Earth Day

I'm finally getting around to telling about my visit to Duluth for Easter. I got in on Monday of Easter Week. Everyone had to work and go to school so it was me and Nu every day until 2:30 when Ves and Essie got home. We got up every morning at 6:30 and they were out the door by 7:45. I brushed hair while they ate their cereal, Essie's long beautiful honey-colored hair and Nuie's blonde thatch like a cute little haystack. She has a patch of gnarly tangled hair in the back of her head that will not brush out no matter what. After they left, Nu and I would watch Sesame Street Spoofs for an hour or so until she got tired of it and would shut off the TV and close the doors herself. Then we got out the stroller and made our way through the alleys to the Co-op to shop for dinner. I got lucky with the weather – many days were sunny and spring-like with shrinking snow every day. The amount of snow was huge though – up to the eaves of the garages. We spent a lot of time on the back porch basking in the sun. After lunch, Nu would bring out pillows and blankets from the house to make herself a nest and go off to sleep. She's almost potty trained and would say urgently that she had to go and would quickly tippy toe (so cute!) to the bathroom shutting the door for 'privacy.' I would stay outside the door and ask if she was done and get permission to come in and wipe. Poor girl would let her skirt fall down into the toilet so we would need a wardrobe change after. We had a really nice time together and I'm so glad I got that time to be with her since she will only be a delightful 2 ½ for a short time longer. After 2:30 Es was home and I focused more on her while Nu wanted to be with her mom. Essie and I looked at Barbie movies and Tumble books on the computer and just kinda hung out. One day she brought home a kachina – I was so impressed – it was just like a real kachina even decorated with feathers. The teacher had typed out the story – the name was "Ananas and she was an Indian girl who lived in the pueblo and went to dances and her her own drum." There was more but that's what I remember. It was amazing !! On Saturday everyone was home, Gracie came over and we dyed Easter eggs. On Easter Sunday we had a great brunch with all the Kershaws at Ves and Jer's house. I acted as Ves' sous chef and we turned out a beautiful brunch of frittata, asparagus, polenta with maple syrup, potatoes, bacon and mimosas and Sandy brought coffee and orange rolls. It was delicious. We had an egg hunt out back and then just visited. Sean and Tim are so nice and got very involved with giving Ves and Jer advice on their kitchen renovation. I had a nice talk with Vince about books. Ves and Es played hooky the next day, a beautiful sunny day and we took a drive up the North Shore to have lunch at the Scenic Café. Es was disappointed we couldn't walk on the shore but it was piled up with ice. Since I've been home they've gotten another few feet of snow- twice – shut the town down.......The trip back was pretty dramatic, missed my connection throuth Mpls and got routed through Atlanta ! I visited every time zone but PST twice that day, spent the whole day riding in a plane through a major storm in the South, bumping along, and finally got home at 8:30, seven hours late !!

August 16, 2013

Got back earlier this week from ten days with the girls. Duluth was beautiful and lush but so cool for summer, we only got a tiny bit of swimming in and that was disappointing. Ves and Jer are almost finished with their new kitchen and it is so elegant and great to cook in. I was there for Nuie's 3rd birthday on August 11. She got some great presents, from me a rapunzel dress from the Little Dress Up Shop and from her Mom and Dad a kitchen that fit right into the corner of the dining room. Ves brought down a little table and chairs from upstairs. Nu was so cute bustling around with her oven mitt, slamming the microwave and putting dishes on the table. She's such a fastidious little person.

When we sit down to eat she says "napkin, please" and wipes off her fingers and dabs her lips throughout the meal. I made a kid dinner for them on the Saturday I took care of them all day while Ves and Jer were down in the Cities for Selene's memorial service. The dinner was hot dogs, mac n'cheese and green peas, their favorites. We started to eat when Nu says "we forgot to do thankfuls." So we all held hands and she said "I'm thankful that Baba is here to make us this delicious dinner." I had a moment of horror one day when I saw Nuie trying to carry the clothes basket up the cellar stairs. She was about halfway up and struggling. She would have been badly hurt if she had tumbled backward. Fortunately I got there in time. We all lectured her about not climbing the stairs with anything in her hands. After the third lecture, she said "okay, let's not talk about that anymore!" Ves just put a post on FB about asking Nu what kind of music she would like to hear. She said "quiet music so the neighbors won't think we're crazy." Sandy replied "spoken like a true Midwesterner." Although I should add that Sil can be a little stinker as when she hid the car keys when we went camping. Jer left them on the front seat and they disappeared. Apparently this happens because both Ves and Jer immediately turned to Nuie and asked where are the keys? She giggled mischievously and wouldn't tell. Ves found them later at home in a camp bag and in the meantime Ves had another set so we weren't stranded in Herbster. It's a testament to Ves and Jer's parenting that they didn't overreact and punish her. How could you though, she's such a darling. I told Jer he needed to take a little responsibility there leaving keys on the frontseat in reach of a three-year old who likes to hide things. She loves to give presents esp to her sister in the bath tub. Esme told me on the q.t. that is her favorite game in the tub. She drapes the wash cloth over the side of the tub and places a toy in it, wraps it up and presents it to her sister. Essie unwraps and makes ooh ahh noises while Nuie cocks her head and smiles and smiles, clapping her hands together, then does another present. She and Essie are really close – they sleep together like two puppies. There seems to be a good balance of power between them even though Es is three years older. Es has a temper and one day they were playing outside when she exploded. All we could hear was "you're NOT cooperating" and see Es throw herself down on the grass wailing. Nuie came into the kitchen and said coyly "Rayray mad." She wasn't the least bit upset by it! I can certainly sympathize with Es' temper since I have one myself. Now that I'm home, I keep seeing Essie's face as she looked one morning when she came downstairs for breakfast. She was all tender looking and her eyes were like big pansies. Hard to describe but I'll never forget it. The many faces of Es. She asked me to tell her a story so I gave them Jurassic Park complete with the T Rex pounding down on the explorers with his big teeth and breath reeking of rotten meat, etc. I really hammed it up and she loved it. I told her about playing spin the bottle when I was 10 or 11 and she was riveted with that, asked a lot of questions, most notably, what do you do if the bottle points at someone you don't want to kiss?

Later Es paid me the biggest compliment: I said something joking about me being boring and she said with big eyes "Oh no, Baba, you're NEVER boring." Ves tells me that Es said something similar to her – Ves said "oh, I must be the worst mother in the world" and Essie said "You're the BEST mother in the world !" Nu and Essie both laughed and laughed when I couldn't understand something they said, which happened a lot, and I would say what I thought I heard, making it as silly as possible. Essie has a habit of not saying "r" clearly so when she said something like "fwee fwoggie" I would copy her and then she would get all indignant and say, "no, Baba, it's 'free froggie' very emphatically like I was the one making the mistake. She's a very sensitive girl – we all watched a horrible movie "Franken Weenie" a cartoon about a dog brought back to life. When it was finally over, Essie burst into tears and threw herself into her Dad's arms. I hope she never loses that ….

October 8, 2013

Email from Avesa on the new kittens:

"Yes, little Tina and Maya (or JoJo, there's some debate about the name for the black and white tabby) are wrestling on the couch behind me. They're SO adorable and playful. We drove up north of Hibbing today, to meet their family, a very nice Mennonite couple in their fifties with weathered and warm faces. We also met the mom, a very sweet and mellow long-haired calico. She played with the girls by pinning them down and licking them all over. Their nose kiss goodbye was fairly heartbreaking. Then we loaded them into the car in a cage we borrowed from Ama and Pop Pop, but the girls fought so fiercely (play fighting gone too far) that I had to separate them, so they took turns laying on my lap. Tina stretched out her whole tiny body in the sun for most of the ride.

Unfortunately, just five minutes home, one reached up and attacked Silvi's leg in play. There was a little scratch in her skin and now she's traumatized and won't walk near them, and has been sitting on tables and asking us to carry her from one room to the next. Poor thing said, "I want to take the cats home now." Then Essie came home from school and just melted with joy. She has been making them little beds and toys and introducing them to all of her stuffed animals. My allergies are so so. I have noticed a few minutes where my throat kind of closes up, but I am also getting over a cold. I hope it's not going to be an issue.

Oh my god, they're curled into one little ball right now. I have to take a picture and send it to you."

January 2014 Visit

Ves and the girls arrived Saturday afternoon the 4th and stayed until the 14th. Jer flew in on the Wednesday. We did a fun round of tourist activities like the zoo, Old Town, museums, visit to Alana's farm and best of all, the dances at Jemez Pueblo (Walatowa). We saw buffalo, antelope, deer, eagle and a beautiful girl wearing a white buckskin dress dancing a floating sort of dance up the middle of the plaza to a chief with big headdress surrounded by drummers and singers. It was really special and I hope the girls will remember it always.

Folding towels with Silvi later I told her she was a very good big girl and she said … "I'm a fabulous girl" Next morning walking through the house looking around, she said "this is a dream house.' With Essie nearby, she told me " I'm going to be on the 'tage' when I grow up" I said "the tage?" Essie, looking bored says "she means 'the stage.' This from a three-year old? What! I should have asked more questions at that point! I must remember to do that in future (rather than just gape). The two girls are so cute together. Silvi calls Essie "RayRay" and Essie calls Silvi "Newbo." Silvi told me they plan to always sleep together. Now and then Silvi goes all quiet and Es told me she's in "Nibbit" mode. The girls like the 'finer things' I gave them juice one morning in thin champagne glasses and they wanted to drink out of those glasses all the time after that.

Poor Es had to do homework every day since she was taking off school for the visit. She's not exactly excited about it since like any normal child, she would rather be doing anything else than homework. I was surprised at the level she was already at for a mid-term first grader, but Ves tells me that she's working hard to keep up. Where Essie excels (just like her mom did) is creative stuff. Es invented a dessert (yogurt, blueberries, walnuts, maple syrup) that she was so proud of. It was really touching to see how happy this made her. Hope she never forgets that.

Dave and I have been making this dessert for ourselves ever since. It's a good one, Es !! I made an art desk for them to work at while they were here, covered with colorful posterboard and stocked with all kinds of crayons, pencils, watercolors, workbooks and lots of paper. The two of them worked away at their creations for hours on end. Essie was really into fossils and found many right around here. She and her dad explored a deep arroyo not far from the house and found all kinds of great fossils.

April 21, 2014

Back last week from Duluth with yet another streaming cold. This is three for three visits. But nevertheless, had a delightful time with the girls who were on spring break while Ves and Jer had to work. So I had them all to myself a lot of the time ! We had two lovely spring-like days which melted a lot of the massive amounts of snow and opened up the sidewalks. Nib, Ray and I took out the stroller and headed down to Lakewalk one day and went to McDonalds for lunch. A treat for the girls. I love the nicknames they have for one another: Nib is Silvia and Ray (or RayRay) is Essie. They're like the Mitford girls – the Kershaw girls. We played outside all day on both of those beautiful days. Essie put on the 'Olympics' out front with many exciting events racing up and down the sidewalk, the lava jump, the bike races, the razor races, hopscotch. I sat on the porch steps and announced each event, cheering away. The energy level is mind-boggling. Another game that Essie loved was Scavenger Hunt. I drew up a list of 10 items – we had inside and outside games – then she ran off and found them. I checked them off when she returned then rewarded her with a snack. I tried to give her a quarter for one game and she turned it down – wanted the snack. My conversation with Silvie about food: I said she was eating a lot (as I fed her the 6th cracker with butter) and she said "I want to grow....but bagels and cookies make you fat." So I said, "what's good food?" and she said "carrots and broccoli" Three years old and she knows that!!! On one cold morning I told her she had to put on a scarf so I found one in the boxes and wrapped it around her neck. She said "I look good in a scarf" I wonder if Ves ever told her that? (no – I asked). Silvia has no problems in the confidence area, and she'll tell you off in a minute, as they say in Bermuda. Sandy says she's 'brutally honest.' I asked her if she would miss me when I went home and and she said "Um, actually, no."

On Saturday, our luck ran out with the good weather so I took the girls shopping at the mall, driving their new car which was a first. We had a ball, we visited every kid's clothing store there, bought really cute outfits and stayed within the $30 each budget. They rode the carousel twice and threw pennies in the wishing well. I gave them each a penny and told them to think of a wish and it had to be secret. They took this very seriously and took their time, then flung the penny in. We had lunch at Culver's and ate so much they were laid flat out on the booth seat.

Ves told about a story that Es wrote recently. It was a retelling of the Cinderella story in which Cindy is a giant Cheerio. Ves said Es had even drawn a picture of her in her wedding dress as a Cheerio. Then the prince had a big bowl of Cheerios and ate her up.

Tina and JoJo, the kitties are now about six months old and part of the family. Jer says he's not that attached to them but one night Tina didn't come in after dark and Jer was out with his headlamp on searching for her. He found her at the top of the big cedar tree next door and coaxed her down to a lower branch which he was able to pull down and grab her. So sad but since I left the neighbor Bill has cut down this wonderful tree, Everyone's upset about it, including me and I don't even live there. It was a beauty.

Esme and Silvi with Avesa and grandpop Dave

Avesa with Esme and Silvi

Picnic time with Silvers and Essie on their back porch

Dad Jeremy Kershaw with Esme

Avesa reading to Essie

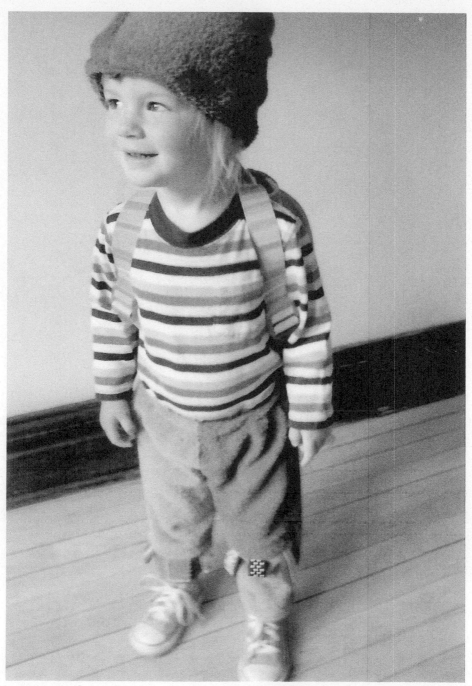

Esme the toddler

Silvi

Esme

Nuie at Christmas

Silvi at the beach

Esme at the beach in Duluth

Hobbling along on broken leg in St. Georges

CHAPTER 10

Bermuda Trip

June 30, 2016:

Met the girls at the airport, so happy to see them. Silvi had a cast on her wrist but Ves said it was minor and she had a swim cast so not to worry and that worked out well over the next two weeks. I was dazed from all night travel on the JetBlue redeye, not much sleep. They were coming in from Toronto on Air Canada and had spent the night at a hotel in Toronto. This was the start of our nostalgia visit, for me marking the 50th anniversary of my first stay in Bermuda and for Avesa, the wonderful summers she spent as a teen staying with her grandmother in Spanish Point. Bermuda is a very special place for both of us. There's no place else in the world like it.

We got a cab to St. Georges and checked in to our sleek apartment on Water Street, just steps from King's Square. We had lunch at the place downstairs and me, craving a fish sandwich, ordered one that was billed as a "fresh and creative approach." It was like mashed potatoes on a bun with avocado cream on top, just awful. I told the server I couldn't eat the rest. She walked us to the back deck and threw it into the water where it was swarmed by fish and disappeared in seconds. Glad someone liked it. Back at the apartment we got on our suits and headed off to Tobacco Bay for a snorkel. St. Georges is so charming, full of colorful old historic buildings with flowering trees and vines spilling over stone walls, we were dazzled. Then disaster struck by the old abandoned church. I stepped off a steep curb and fell in the street, bloody elbow and leg hurt but me in denial we carried on to the beach and had a nice swim until early evening. When it was time to leave I could not put any weight on my leg. A nice hefty Bermudian man helped me into a taxi and off we went to the Lamb Foggo Clinic in St. Davids. Nothing broken and for $777 I got an x-ray, a knee wrap, a cane and some pain pills. No waiting though, and the doctor was a bluff droll character, light skinned with a Scottish name and accent. He said it was a deep bruise. Hopefully I can get some money back from my insurance. I joked with them that I had hit the lucky jackpot with three 7s and they laughed. That was it for me though. It was bad, Ves had to help me to the bathroom in the middle of the night. She's a light sleeper and would spring awake poor girl when I stirred. I told her I was sorry for the bother and she said not to worry that it gave her the opportunity to show me how much she loved me. That meant a lot!! In return I didn't complain (much) and did my best to keep up my spirits.

Friday, July 1

I had to spend the day in bed so the girls went to Tobacco Bay and had fun. They made friends with a little girl and her family who were staying at the St. George's Club.

Saturday, July 2

I was a little better so we went back to Tobacco Bay in a taxi driven by a foxy young Bermudian.. I told her there were no female taxi drivers back in the day when I worked for Island Taxi and she said there are some now and I said the world's a better place. We had a fun day there, lots of snorkeling which Silvi took to right away. It was so cute to see her flippering around. I went out with her side by side and she would take my hand now and then but she wasn't frightened and was thrilled to see the fish and one time a squad of little squid. Esme was scared of it but I predict she'll be back. Floating weightless in the water was the best I would feel for the duration. Ves snorkeled around the big rock and reported that it looked much better and healthier than in the past with brain coral and big purple fans. Around noon a party bus pulled up and the party was on all afternoon. Lots of great reggae music with a DJ. It was so fun to hear that Bermuda accent again.

Sunday, July 3

I was hurting and needed a day off so the girls took the bus to Crystal Caves and came back around noon – Ves got some beautiful pictures. We went to a very nice fancy brunch at a restaurant that used to be the Carriage House on Water Street and then walked to Kings Square where a Portuguese Festival was carrying on. I asked if Elsie Martin was there and someone told me she was 'away' at a relative's funeral in the States. Sorry I missed her. We got some ice cream and retired to the quiet of Somer's Park. It started getting dark and we decided it was time to go, getting to the gate just as the gribbly warden was locking up. The park had some amazing tropical trees I've never seen before, very tall with folds in the trunk big enough to hide a Silvi.

Monday, July 4

We checked out of our neato apt, left our bags at the shop downstairs and got a cab to Tobacco Bay. Ves got me a lounge chair and set it in a patch of shade. Then along came a woman my age with a cane and her daughter lugging over a lounge chair. I had a patch of shade next to me to I told her to put her chair down there and that's how I met Hillary from London who was also in Bermuda for a nostalgia trip with her kids, Camille and her son Cayenne. We had a lot in common. She had been in Bermuda at the Bio Station in the 70s. We talked a bunch and when we left after lunch to catch the ferry to Hamilton we agreed to meet up again after they moved down to Paget staying at Newstead. We took a cab to get our bags and get to the ferry station. Poor Ves was the total pack animal loaded up with all the bags. The ferry along the North Shore to Dockyard was scenic. At Dockyard we had to transfer to the Coralita to Hamilton. Ves kinda lost it for a brief moment with all the bags, not like her. I felt bad I couldn't help. At Hamilton she parked me at Allbouys Point with the bags and they all took off for Miles Market. I was really regretting bringing that totally unneccssary second bag. But we got a cab to Scarrington, Middle Road, Paget and that was the last we had to deal with the goddam luggage. When we left ten days later, I ditched the old dirty bag and left a hat and flippers for the next person.

We were thrilled with the cottage, Garden View. As we stepped over the old cedar doorstep we could smell that unique Bermuda smell. It was clean and nicely furnished with all the mod cons as the Brits say. Our landlord, Greg Soares was 'away' and had arranged with Ves to Face Time when we got in, the key was under the mat. He walked her through the house via the tablet and told her all she needed to know. That night was Fourth of July. After Ves' good dinner we went out on the porch and to our amazement a big fireworks display went up from the direction of Elbow Beach at sunset. Ves and I warbled the Star Spangled Banner and the girls looked at us in amazement.

Tuesday, July 5

We set out for Warwick Long Bay and Jobson's Cove, using our $200 seven day bus/ferry pass. Ves scouted ahead with a trip to the grocery store and came back very worried about the dangerous gauntlet we would have to run to get to the bus stop. The walk down Scarrington Hill and along the road was agonizing for me compounded by the constant fear for the girls getting hit by a car. The road is narrow, many blind corners lined with stone walls and we had to walk single file with cars and trucks whizzing by inches away. The girls were scared. If there's anything I could say about Bermuda for the worse it's that increased pace of life and speeding cars, not at all like the old days with cars leisurely driving at 20 mph. The old taxis were open air with ball fringe all around the canopy; today's taxis are air conditioned high tech behemoths. Bermuda has caught up with the rest of the world in that regard. On the plus side, the internet speed was blinding, way better than what we have here at home. We had Roku in the cottage with everything from Netflix to Youtube to amazon available. So back to the beach, my favorite beach Warwick Long Bay. I had a hard time getting in and out with the surf, Ves helped me with an arm around her shoulders. One time though I was getting really pruned and Ves wasn't around so I tried to get out on my own and got tumbled in the surf, suit full of sand, trying to crawl out. Then Ves showed up and a couple other people on the beach helped me out. Man, the injury has been a humbling experience and a foretaste of what real old age will be like. Ves brought me Tupperwares of water to pour down the inside of my suit to get the sand out. Es and Silvi surprised me – they didn't care much for Jobson's but loved the surf on Warwick Long Bay. They were in the water for HOURS and made little friends most every day. Essie was crazy about doing flips and handstands in the water, she didn't like snorkeling, it kinda scared her and back at the cottage she would watch videos of 'barracuda attack' on her Mom's tablet. The tablet was a life saver. We didn't have a phone, and the girls got to face time with their Dad a few times.

Wednesday, July 6

My leg was killing me and I couldn't face the bus trip so stayed in and the girls took the bus to Church Bay which is way too steep for me to maneuver with the cane. They had a great time and so did I back at the cottage reading the Bermuda library the Soares furnished. I especially liked Ann Spurlings book "Bermuda: Nine Parishes" full of stories and beautiful photos of the island. I liked the Bermuda Heritage series too. I saw a photo of Maria Flood, a plump and pretty Portagee woman and her tall, skinny husband posed behind a large dead hog they were getting ready to butcher. Pat later told me that Eric Flood's father was a well known butcher for Miles Market so I bet that couple was Brenna's grandparents. I emailed her about our trip and told her she really needed to go to Bermuda to reconnect with her Flood family. I hope she does.

Thursday, July 7

We all went to Horseshoe Bay. Ves rented a lounger and umbrella for me and we had hot dogs, burgers and ice cream for lunch. Es was in heaven...she said that Horseshoe was her favorite beach. After lunch, Ves and girls walked down to the far end of Horseshoe and around the big rocks to Brenna's old favorite beach that Essie named Pony Beach. I'm sure it has an official name but we didn't know it. It was so great to just lounge in that gorgeous turquoise water.

Friday, July 8

We took the bus to the Aquarium which didn't hold a candle to the Toronto aquarium the girls had seen on the trip out. The highlight was the bridge over Flatts Inlet right next to the Aquarium where we saw all kinds of fish and a turtle in the wild. On the way back we got off the bus at Shelly Bay thinking we'd have a swim there but it was way too rough and windy so we packed it in and headed home.

It was a gorgeous blue sky day but a stiff NW wind was predicted so we looked for a protected beach and that was Mangrove Bay in Somerset, a long and scenic bus ride. When we got there the bay was full of anchored boats but calm with a shallow grassy bottom. We were excited to see several turtles swimming around and some small barracudas. Unfortunately, the narrow beach was full of broken glass and Ves did not have beach shoes. The girls kept on their flippies in the water and I wore my smelly beach shoes. So on the advice of a nice local woman we walked to Somerset Long Bay along a quiet road lined with oleander, hibiscus and beautiful houses, notably Cambridge House. There was a big grass field with local families grilling and a lovely beach but also full of broken glass. We stayed, the girls made friends and had fun in the water. It was a beach for locals and everyone was picking up broken glass and putting it in a pile. No one got their feet cut I'm happy to report. Somerset was different, no tourists to speak of, kind of run down in places but charming. It's considered "the country" and there were lots of small fields under cultivation, roosters crowing and a horse staked out for grazing. This was another sad change in Bermuda which used to have riders and horse drawn carriages and sulkies on the roads everywhere. I didn't see one. I asked a cab driver about it and he told me there was a runaway carriage horse on Front Street. No one got badly hurt but ever since, the only carriages are special order for weddings and such.

Ves got in touch with Camille at Newstead and we made arrangements to meet there for brunch. It was a short walk to Newstead but I couldn't do it with my leg, so we booked a cab. Greg Soares turned us on to this app called Hitch that was a lifesaver since we didn't have a phone. It took credit cards too which was good for our dwindling cash. It was cool – it showed you on the map where the nearest cabs were and how many minutes away. This was the last day for our bus/ferry pass so we planned to take the ferry across the harbor after lunch and look around Hamilton. I was shocked at the changes in Newstead. I remembered it as an elegant old fashioned hotel but this place was space age with walls of thick glass and chrome. The dining room was laid out with the most lavish buffet. Essie and Silvi's eyes were big as saucers. It was astounding. We had to wait a bit for Hillary and her crew so we inspected the displays laden with salads, sushi, desserts, soups, entrees and an omelet and waffle stations. Silvi and Es picked out the desserts they were going to get and then got busy with their colors and designing until they arrived. They are the busiest kids, the whole trip when we weren't at the beach they were working away at their paper doll designer collection and talking pretend 'fashion designer' to one another. It was so funny to listen in. Ves said that this was the most they had played together in a long time.

Hillary arrived looking glamorous in a blue batik dress with long twirly blue wooden earrings. She wore an amulet bag around her neck and before we ate, she showed me all the various crystals and stones she had in it. I told her she would be right at home in Santa Fe. She had this one amulet on a chain that she held over food to see if it would agree with her (I thought that was a bit over the top). Her grandson Cayenne looked at his phone the whole time, listening in on our conversation. He's 17 with a warm shy smile. Ves carried on a lively conversation with Camille who is 38 and works as a fashion buyer in London. They both looked just like their grandmother but with beautiful brown skin. Hillary told me her father, an Orthodox Jew, almost disowned her when she told him she was having a baby with a black man and really lost it when she told him she was marrying one when Camille was a baby. She lives alone now near Camille in London and has a boyfriend who looks after her too. She helps Camille run their business Pink Ribbon Lingerie for post-mastectomy. We ate and talked for about three hours, exchanged contact info and finally said good-bye to take the ferry to Hamilton. The dock was just below the hotel. It was tough for me to navigate the moving deck getting on and off but I did it. This disability is a new experience for me. I sure will appreciate the simple act of walking when I get better. I was so afraid that I would fall again or get knocked down. In Hamilton, I needed to sit so found a bench by the ferry terminal while the girls took off exploring. I met some lovely people – a Mrs. Lightbourne from Flatts and her 'second son' who is a tugboat captain dressed in an immaculate white uniform. This was the silver lining to getting injured: I met and talked with so many great Bermudians. They are truly a special people. They all gave me advice on my leg from "soak it in the sea" to a poultice made from mashed up "Match Me If You Can" leaves in bay rum. Ves bought me the bay rum at Robertsons in St. Georges and the girls picked me the leaves so I did the poultice three times and it did make the leg feel better but not a total cure.

Monday, July 11

Silvi elected to stay home with me while Ves and Essie walked Tribe Road No. 4 to Elbow Beach. I would have loved to go with them but Silvers and I had a very nice day. We watched "Home" which was just terrific and had pizza for lunch, her favorite. I like spending time with the girls separately. They are embroiled in the older sister/younger sister dynamic so it's nice to be with them alone to see what they have to say for themselves. When together Silvi would say things to Essie like, "I love you very, very much but I don't think you love me at all." Essie would protest yes, she did, and Silvi would say 'but you're always mad at me.' And so on. Ves was happy that they played together so well the entire trip.

Tuesday, July 12

Our first and only rainy day. We took a cab to Hamilton and had lunch at The Spot then went to the movies to see "Dory." The lunch was very good and not expensive since The Spot is a locals restaurant. One woman on the bus told me about a $15 hot dog at the Fairmont Princess. Almost everything in Bermuda is double what it is at home with the exception of drugs. Ves got me a big box of ibuprofen for only $5.00 at Robertsons.

Wednesday, July 13

Our last day for the beach. We went to Horseshoe again and discovered our mistake too late: Tuesday and Wednesday is when the cruise ship people come to Horseshoe. Ves dubbed it "The Rookery." It was okay though even if it was more like Coney Island than Bermuda. We were lucky to get a lounger with umbrella. The sun is so intense you must have shade. Then an elderly Russian woman was leaving and gave us her lounger and umbrella 'for the children'. Ves said she regretted not buying an umbrella when we first arrived....we saw in the Royal Gazette ad insert they they were on sale somewhere. We had to leave Horseshoe just as it was getting nice and not so hot. Es wanted to stay, we all did, but we had to get back to the cottage and get ready to go out. If I lived in Bermuda, I would do what the locals do and go to the beach in the early evening.

That night we went to Harbour Nights in Hamilton and met up with Hillary and gang, had a bite to eat and then heard the intoxicating drums of the Gombeys so we hurried on over to watch them. Ves stood the girls up on a wall so they had a clear view. It was exciting. When we got home, Es got her Mom's tablet and looked up an image for a Gombey and got busy making one like a paper doll. We left early that night since Silvi was running a fever and not feeling well. That night it topped out at 103 and we were very concerned. Ves gave her some antibiotic since Essie had had strep just before the trip and that may have been what Silvi had. She was better in the morning but not 100% and the fever came back but not high. I think she was fine by the time they got home.

Thursday, July 14

Our last day. We left at 10:00 a.m. for the airport. The night before we had gotten a taxi with Sgt. Astwood, moonlighting on his job as a policeman. He was a really cordial and handsome Bermudian. We mentioned that we were leaving the next day so he promised to be there at 10:00 and he was right on time. He was the best taxi driver we had and he only charged us $32, half what I thought it would be. We only had one bad driver and that was from Horseshoe the day before. I think he was mentally ill - ranted loudly about foreigners taking all the best jobs, bread was $7 and rents were too high, etc.. Ves said that man should not be working in the tourist industry. You run into very few bad eggs like that though. I remember back in the day when I worked for Island Taxi, there were always a few malcontents. I always asked the taxi drivers if they remembered Ralph Terceira and Island Taxi and a few did; I was surprised that more didn't. I always sat up front with the driver to chat and ask questions.

At the airport, we had to check in separately and agreed to meet upstairs in the restaurant. I never saw them again ! We didn't know that Air Canada was a separate concourse. Oh well, I'll see them at Halloween in Duluth but it was sad not to be able to say good-bye. One good thing: I finally got the fish sandwich I was craving and it was the best I've ever had, big juicy chunks of fresh fish with lettuce and tomato on toast. It was sooo good.

The trip back reminded me of what Mark Twain said long ago: "Bermuda is paradise, but you have to go through hell to get there." I was supposed to get in at 10:00 p.m. and it was 1:30 a.m. when poor exhausted Dave picked me up. It was worse for Ves and the girls. They had to sleep on the floor of the airport in Minneapolis because they had missed the last shuttle to Duluth. They didn't get in until 10 the next morning.

I think we all had a really good time. Ves tells me the girls are regaling Jer with stories of all they saw and did. I had a good time too even with the banged up leg. I agree with Mark Twain who said "When I die, I want to go to Bermuda."

Lunch at Newstead with new friends from London: from left:: Silvi, Esme, me, Avesa, Hilary Johnson, her grandson Kayenn and his mom Camille.

Our airbnb home in Bermuda "Garden View" Paget

My sister Pat's and my old home in Bermuda in 1967-68 "Scarrington" Paget.

Silvi at Warwick Long Bay

Esme at Church Bay

Bermuda cottage

My daughter's house.

CHAPTER 11

My Daughter's House

My daughter's house is 100 years old. It's a little house that dwells beneath a mighty maple tree on a quiet leafy street in Duluth, Minnesota. Just a half block away and down a steep flight of rough stone steps is Chester Creek Park, described once as "a primeval forest in the heart of the city." It's a lush glen of towering white pines and thimbleberry bushes, clear cold water tumbling down towards Lake Superior over rocks and waterfalls pausing only at swimming holes that lure plunging dogs and hot children on summer days. This tree and this glen I think are what sold the kids on this humble Sears Roebuck catalog house ten years ago when they tied the knot. It was ideal and affordable for a young active family with two youngsters on the way. Since then Ves and Jer have made the kitchen elegant and modern, thanks to Ikea, and they've replaced old glazed windows with new insulated ones. They came down from Ely every weekend when they were working up there as outfitters the summer they bought the house and worked hard to refinish the beautiful maple floors that were under ugly old carpets. A few light switches are right out of Victrola days, fat Bakelite buttons that take some pushing. Otherwise, the house is what it always was and continues to be. It's a dear place, one that I've become very fond of over many visits.

Let's take a tour: from the sidewalk out front (that may sport a chalk-drawn hopscotch on its tree-heaved surface) we ascend the front steps to the porch. Many summer evenings are spent sitting on these steps watching the neighborhood posse of kids skate and bike up and down the block, screeching and laughing. It's a classic Midwestern porch with a wooden swing attached to the ceiling with hooks and 70s era classroom desk for outdoor play. I first laid eyes on Essie on this swing; she was zipped up in her Dad's jacket with just her little face peeking out like a baby owl, six weeks old. Her Dad looked like an angry hawk (I realized I had my work cut out for me, oh dear…but ten years on, we're good). Avesa's stone pineapple from San Francisco welcomes guests to the front door. There's a small patch of grass out front and a shady garden of Hosta plants. A bird's nest is tucked under an eave. We've had many happy hours sitting in the swing reading or enjoying the sunset which makes the porch glow with color. Our young entrepreneur Essie and her helper Nibbit ran their nail salon and rock shop from this porch. A passing neighbor wanted to buy a rock but had no money with her so our girl sold her the rock on credit. Next day, Es recruited me to walk with her to the neighbor's house to collect, and the promised envelope containing $1 was waiting on the porch. I was so impressed with such good business sense from an eight-year old.

We step up to the stout rusty red front door (which may be original) and push the 70's era door bell. Avesa or Jer will come to the door and invite us into the living room. From the doorway we see seemingly one big room that serves as living and dining room (there is a slender defining column between the rooms) Three large double hung windows at the end of the dining room give onto the back porch and down the long narrow backyard to the garage and alley. We may see the family cats Tina and JoJo sleeping on the radiator cabinet that Jer built under the windows. Tina is a droll little cupcake of a Calico cat. Her sister JoJo is gray and white, shy and sweet. Next to them on the shelf are a few plants, notably an aloe for kitchen burns. In the corner Jer has installed coat hooks at kid level and colorful boxes for gloves and hats. The dining room has a long plain mahogany table that is art central. The walls are papered with the girls' work in crayon, pen and watercolor, cardboard and fabric. Their parents wisely limit screen time and the girls are told "do something creative" and boy, do they ever. The production is prodigious. Esme excels at design and says (at 9) that she wants to be a fashion designer. Silvia at 6 does not have a designated grown-up goal yet other than 'scatology' (!!) but she produces nice art and she knows it.

This is a house meant to be lived in by a family with two active youngsters, very few knickknacks or frills. There's a homely brown sofa and a comfy round rug, a cabinet containing the TV, turntable and cd player. Some artwork on the walls, mostly photos from the very talented Jeremy and a nude watercolor by Avesa's brother Alec. There's a wooden folk art northern pike on the stereo speaker that I've always admired. A large red wooden toy box contains legos, Lincoln logs, plastic animals, cars, little people and all the things the girls need to build towns, houses and farms with a running dialogue that is often hilarious.

The kitchen is separated from the dining room by a spacious peninsula of a counter with cabinets underneath on the dining room side holding cookbooks, linens and the girls' art supplies. The surface is a pleasing dark gray formica. There's a deep enamel sink and a clever roll-out drawer that holds the trash and recycle bins as well as a drawer for various food storage items. The kitchen was remodeled a few years ago and has contributed a great deal to Avesa's happiness in the house. I always cook when I visit and the kitchen is a pleasure to work in.

There are glass-fronted cabinets and a good gas stove with a capacious hood and a new stainless steel refrigerator. On the walls are Jer's photos, currently of bar signs from Ely, Minnesota. I say 'currently' because the kids are constantly changing things up and rearranging things in their house. Off the kitchen are the cellar steps, at the bottom, a pantry with garlic and herbs drying on the walls. Let's pause on the steps and breathe in the aroma of a thousand delicious dinners. For some reason, these gustatory ghosts linger on the steps. I'm always taken back to my grandmother Gammy's kitchen. I lived with her when I was Silvi's age and can still remember the wonderful food she made, pork chops, fried chicken, mashed potatoes and gravy, luscious apple pies and dumplings. Ves and Jer bake bread so that delectable fragrance is added to the mix. The cellar has a bathroom, the "man can" as well as Jer's bike shop. There are two rooms for storage, a washer and dryer, the kitty litter boxes and beds. I've crept down the stairs in the middle of the night to use the toilet and there's Tina and JoJo curled up together in one bed as cozy as can be. Tina will come into the shower when I'm in it and scoot around the edges heedless of getting wet. Must be a Calico thing. Let's head back into the living room and up the stairs to the bedrooms.

To the right of the front door is a staircase leading to the second floor. First a step up to a landing with coat hooks and a framed mirror we gave Avesa years ago that looks so good there it looks like it came with the house. Then up the stairs to the bedrooms and bath. The bathroom is painted a delightful golden shade, plastic tubs of bath toys ready for play. So much enjoyment watching the girls play in the bath…until the dreaded hair washing. It's so endearing to see them wrap their peachy sweet little bodies in terrycloth robes after the bath and rush across the hall to their room. Next to the door Essie has posted rules for getting up in the morning: first, 'Wake up, Deal with it.' The girls' room changes more than any other room in the house. Every time I visit, there's a sea change in that room. For me, there's such a different perspective of time from one end of life to the other. For me at 70, two years goes by like a snap of the fingers. For the girls, it's glacial and as I remember… agonizing… will next year never come?….am I always going to 9 ½? Before too long, the cradle made by Jer's dad and overflowing with stuffed animals will be gone replaced by some teenaged thing. The futon they slept in together has already given way to twin beds. Soon the dress up clothes for fairies and princesses that fill one corner will be gone too. The bookshelf full of kid books will be downsized. We will have many happy memories of those joyful, chaotic years…maybe not the part where they had to be cajoled and bullied to pick up the mess all over the floors. I am always amazed at the speed with which the girls can totally trash a room. Soon enough they will go all tidy on us, maybe even minimalist, who knows. Across the hall is Ves and Jer's room complete with Minnesota drying rack for socks and sweaters. Ves has a tiny alcove study off the bedroom where she works endlessly on her schoolwork. There's a bookcase full of fascinating titles and a door to a balcony that they don't use much. In the winter with the leaves off the trees, you can catch a glimpse of Lake Superior and the Duluth Lift Bridge. You can hear the boat horns from here. Essie surprised me as a toddler when we heard the horns and she said "boat." A true Duluth girl.

Let's head outside. Down the stairs where Silvi as a toddler fell down kabump kabump all the way to the bottom. Ves told me about this on the phone later that day in a remarkably calm voice. She called the doc who told her to just keep an eye on her. She was fine, nothing broken. One of those thankyoulord moments. Out to the back porch through the mudroom where all manner of coats, boots and bicycles are stowed. The porch sits above the backyard by about four feet and is large enough to hold a table and chairs for alfresco dining in the summer. It's a hotpocket facing south and east, a great spot on a sunny winter day for spreading blankets and lounging. Silvi and I did this when Essie was at school one day. Sil brought out some toys and books and we had a luxurious time in the sun. We got some vitamin D that day. I had to be careful she didn't get burned. Then it was 2:30 and time to pick up Es at the bus stop. It's a short walk down 6th . Hugs and home for snacks and play outside in the sun. The backyard is long, narrow and enclosed with a picket fence that Jer built. Ves has created a gem of a rock garden by the back steps and off to the right of the steps by the downspout, a rain garden. Off to the left along the fence she has a garden featuring rhubarb, strawberries, raspberries, garlic and various vegetables in season like lettuce, arugula, peas and chard. There's a coldframe, a grill and a fire ring for outdoor parties in season. In summer, a hammock for lounging and drying towels and bathing suits. Then through an archway that supports a grapevine down a short path lined with tiger lilies and down three stone steps to the garage. There lives the family car, the canoes, lawnmower, tools, etc. The garage gives onto a gravel alley and across the alley are the Fire Woods where Jer has built a magnificent tree house for the neighborhood kids to enjoy.

This concludes th tour of my daughter's home. Two happy kids being brought up by two devoted parents. May they live happily ever after.

Avesa at home

Avesa and her girls on the front porch

The backyard garden

Avesa working at her desk with JoJo the cat

Esme and me in the art studio/dining room.

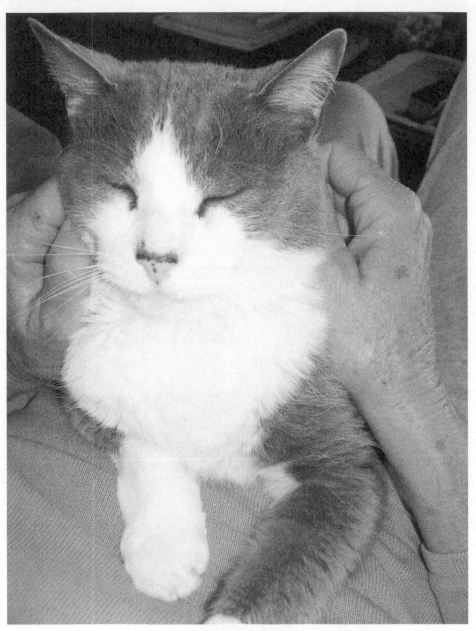

Willie the Gandhi of cats

CHAPTER 12

Cats

This first cat story is not one I remember myself but was told to me by my mother. We were living with my grandparents after the war along with a dozen aunts, uncles and cousins. My young mother put me in a playpen for hours on end in the backyard in the shade of a sycamore tree, just me and my Sears & Roebuck catalog and my doll Audrey. Our sweet cat took me under her protection and brought me a large dead rat for lunch one day. My germaphobic mother was horrified. She came out to find me petting the rat while the cat looked on proudly. She scrubbed down that playpen twice over. I can't say any more about this incident since I was too little to remember, but it was the first time of many times that I got big cat love. My mom always told this story with affection for the kitty whose name I recently found out from my old aunt Winnie was Schicklgruber because the poor cat had a moustache like Hitler. Schicklgruber was Hitler's real name, who knew? A few years later this calico cat had a litter of kittens in the barn that were promptly murdered by the tomcat. My little sister Pat and I were devastated. My grandfather explained to us that this was what tomcats do to kittens sometimes. It was a very sobering event for two little girls. It was around that same time that I saw my first death, a cat who had been hit by a car. His eyes were hanging out of the sockets like two headlights. Horrifying. I can still see it.

When I was six we moved to our own home, a brick row house in the same town as our grandparents. We got a gray tabby cat we named Minnie and she was our cat for the next 20 years. We calculated she had 120 kittens over her career as a mother cat. In those days, the 1950s, people did not get their animals spayed and neutered. We would watch Minnie from the house as she rolled around provocatively on the top of the picnic table while one of her suitors watched from below. Then she would accidentally on purpose tumble onto the ground whereupon the tomcat would make his move. She would disappear for a few days. My mom would always say 'she's gone on her honeymoon.' After her return, we would watch her belly grow larger and larger until it looked like she was full of doorknobs. Then the kittens would be born, sometimes seven in a litter. It was lovely to have kittens around all the time to play with and cuddle. We found homes for every one of them when they were about 8 weeks old and eating on their own. My sister and I had so much fun watching their antics. Once they got up on the dining room table and from there leapt onto the top of my mom's sheer curtains and rode them down on their claws. We thought it was hilarious; my mother was not amused, and the kittens were banned from the house for awhile. What my mother put up with !!

We moved again when I was 12 to a nicer house in the next town of Morton and there… tragedy struck. My little brother had a friend two doors down who was a budding psychopath. He threw all six of our month-old kittens down the cellar steps. When we found them they were bleeding from their mouths and clearly suffering. They had to be put out of their misery. My father couldn't do it, he was the ultimate softie. When we lived with my grandparents, he got a small flock of chickens of his own alongside my grandfather's large flock. He was the city boy married to the country girl and he wanted to try it out. The hens got some sort of deadly disease and had to be destroyed. My dad couldn't do it so he got my two teenaged uncles to chop their heads off, and on the afternoon of the execution, he went upstairs to lie down in the darkened bedroom. I knew this about my dad and I didn't hold it against him. He was all man, but a gentle man. So it was left up to me to put the kittens in a burlap bag and drown them in the creek in the woods across the street. It was awful but I knew it had to be done and without delay. I did it. After that, Minnie did not trust us anymore and had her next litter in the woods. They were feral cats and would not come near any humans. It was a sad time for our family. There were woods and open fields all around so we knew they wouldn't starve. We once saw Minnie drag a huge rat up the driveway to feed the growing kittens. It was so big she had to back up and tug it a foot at a time. Minnie was a formidable cat. We watched her sit at the end of the driveway, calmly licking a paw as the neighbor's Doberman moved in cautiously to attack her. She waited to the last moment without moving a muscle until he got close enough and she then snicked him on the nose with one claw. He ran home howling and she resumed licking her paw like nothing had happened.

Years passed, I left home at 19 to go adventuring to Bermuda, the Bahamas, and Europe. I didn't have another cat until I moved to Wilson, Wyoming for a summer job when I was 24 and going to college in Tucson. At the end of the summer I decided to stay on for another year. It was so beautiful in Jackson Hole I couldn't bear to leave it. During that first summer a couple from San Francisco came to town with their two Russian Blue cats, named Boris and Natasha. These two cats were quite a couple themselves. Boris had suffered an injury across the back of his neck that Natasha had licked and licked until he was healed so the story went. He seemed to have suffered a brain injury as well as he was slow and seemed as dumb as a rock, but nonetheless, Natasha adored him. The human couple found an apartment in the ski village that did not allow pets. They came to us hippies in Wilson and asked if one of us could take the cats. If no one would, they threatened to toss them off the bridge into the Snake River. My boyfriend and I took them in and discovered that Natasha was pregnant. When her kittens came, they were four gorgeous true Russian Blues with coats that looked like sable with silver tipped hairs. Natasha proved to be a good hunter for her kittens and Boris. She brought in big plump marmots and taught her kittens to hunt. I thought this was amazing behavior for a housecat raised in a city apartment. At the end of this wonderful summer, my boyfriend left for home taking one of the kittens with him. I found homes for two and left one with Natasha. I had to make a trip back to Tucson and left cat food and money with my neighbor to take care of the cats. When I returned, they had all vanished. No one knew what had happened. I never saw Boris or the kitten again but one cold stormy winter night I heard scratching on the door. When I opened it, Natasha came bounding in. She was thin and wired. I had a can of cat food left in the cupboard that I opened for her. She wolfed it down, alternating between eating and rubbing against my legs, purring like crazy. She was so excited; our reunion was really touching. I wish she could tell me what happened to Boris and their kitten but of course I could only wonder. The next day I had to go to work and faced the dilemma of what to do with Natasha. I did not have a litter box and had to put her outside during the day while I was gone. After a few days when I came home she would emerge from under the cabin and I realized that she had made a tunnel under the cabin to a spot directly under the warm cookstove. What an amazing survivor she was....until she wasn't. She went off hunting one day in the spring and never returned.

More years passed and I acquired a husband Dave and a darling little daughter Avesa. We were living in Albuquerque while building our adobe home in rural Corrales. Avesa was in kindergarten. We adopted two cats, Crystal and Cholla, I can't remember how or from whom. Cholla disappeared for a few days and we were worried. After the second day I heard a scream from the backyard. Avesa had discovered Cholla in a corner of the yard, just sitting and staring straight ahead like a zombie. When he turned his head you could see that his eye was shattered. The vet pointed out a missing tooth on the opposite side, injuries that indicated he had been hit by a car. Poor Cholla was never the same after that, the blindness in one eye was a serious handicap and within five years we think that he was blindsided by a predator and was gone.

Crystal was a petite tabby with beautiful turquoise eyes. I think she was in the family way when we got her and she surprised us with a litter of kittens before we could get her spayed. We found homes for all the kittens but kept one tabby and named her Margaret. She was our cat for the next 21 years. She was a good solid no nonsense cat. The problem was she was so territorial that we couldn't have another cat in the house without demonic fury. Once, I brought home a young girl kitty named Daphne who needed a new home. Margaret was so vicious to the poor kitty that we had to find her another new home. Crystal in the meantime had disappeared without a trace. Another cat that passed quickly through our lives was Garfield. He was Avesa's cat when she was a young teen. She called him her first boyfriend and he was an orange tabby with the funny personality that orange tabbies all seem to have. He got sick, I took him to the vet and as she examined him she lifted his lip and showed me the dead white color of his gum. She said he had feline leukemia and asked me if she could put him down that day, there was no chance he would survive. I couldn't do that to Avesa, so took him home where he died shortly after. Very sad.

More years passed. As Margaret got older, I thought she might accept another cat. One day, my friend Nancy and I were walking through the park at lunchtime when we saw a young orange tabby going up to people as they passed by- even the FedEx deliveryman. It seemed that he was soliciting someone to take him home. He was so comical and cute about it. No one was taking him up on his offer and then he approached us. He was so charming. I told Nancy that if he was still following us when we got to the street, I would take him home. He was. I took him up to the office and put him in an empty room until it was time to go home. At break time, I visited him with a can of tuna I had in the fridge and a dish of water. I didn't see him in the room, he was hiding somewhere. I called kitty kitty and out he came from behind a slab of sheetrock, giving me the strangest look I've ever seen from a cat. It was a very knowing look, equal parts gratitude and suspicion. It was like "I know I'm going to eat this and then you'll kill me." When I got home, Margaret attacked but he wasn't very intimidated. They worked it out, more or less over the years, but never became friends. There was one terrible incident where Margaret chased him up on a tier of shelves that held my grandmother's precious Japanese lusterware tea set from the thirties. The shelf came down and all was broken but a few pieces. He was forgiven; it wasn't his fault. We named him Lyle and had him for many years. He was the only cat I've ever known who "tail talked." When you talked to him, he would respond by flipping and shaking his tail around in a very expressive manner. He was not an affectionate cat but he made up for it with his comical personality. One day he came home stinking of skunk. The remedy is tomato juice which we didn't have, but we did have a lot of gazpacho that had gone bad. I got him in the shower and lathered him up with the gazpacho and held him under the tap to wash it off, repeated twice. He seemed to understand what I was doing because he didn't put up one bit of struggle and emerged from the shower smelling like olive oil, cucumber and rancid tomato juice - at least it wasn't skunk.

We moved to Placitas from Corrales in 1996. Environmental refugees from Intel Corp. Margaret and Lyle came with us as our cats. Margaret was very old at this point. One afternoon at work I went down to the mailroom to pick up the mail and there was a gray and white kitten about seven months old being spun around on the chair by the drive-up tellers. The poor guy was trying very hard to be a good sport. Another charmer auditioning for a new home. It seened he had been dumped off by someone in the main lobby and one of the tellers had taken him to the back office to figure out what to do with him. I didn't hesitate. I told the tellers that I had dibs on him; I'd be back at five to take him home. When I went back at five, he had thoroughly charmed all the tellers and I had to assert my claim pretty forcefully to get him away. He sat on the passenger seat all the way home and when we got close to home, he got on my lap facing me and jumped up to put his paws on my shoulders and swiped both my cheeks with his whiskers. He was claiming me ! It was really sweet. At home, I took him into the back bedroom and left him there to allow him to introduce himself to Lyle and Margaret. There was never any aggression between them which was unheard of with the fierce Margaret. He became best buddies with Lyle. We would find out as time went by what a peacemaker he was. But in the meantime, he showed us what a hunter he was. That first week we had our Swiss friends visit. Dave stepped outside with Kosta and Willie followed. In the space of 20 minutes, he captured five birds which Dave took from his mouth and released. The guys were impressed, Kosta saying 'ooh lala.' Willie never did this again - I think he was just showing off his skills and proving what a worthy cat he was. His favorite prey turned out to be baby rabbits and during the season he would eat one every day, every bit of the rabbit except for the tiny greenish gall bladder. He started losing weight. Alarmed, we took him to the vet who told us he probably had a fur-lined gut from all the rabbits he ate and couldn't absorb any nutrients, so we had to curb the hunting. He was not a big cat but small and slim with thin silky fur; you wouldn't think he was such a hunter. Wool (nickname) was a very attractive cat. He had a dark batman helmet with a lightning strike feature in the middle of his forehead and two perfectly symmetrical black teardrops in the inner corner of each green eye. The top of his nostrils was outlined with a thin black line. He had a snowy white cape and white socks on his delicate little feet. He looked like a feline superhero. My husband Dave says Willie was his favorite cat ever. He fell asleep on Dave's chest most nights watching TV and would follow us up to bed and burrow under the covers between us in winter. We had Wool for a few years when Bea came on the scene. She was a low slung rough haired little gal who was running away from a bad situation. We took her in and found out soon after the sad story. The wife didn't like her and kept her in the cold dark garage. She escaped and ran down the hill to our house. The husband told us we could keep her and gave us her food and litter box. Bea fell madly in love with Willie. She would pin him down and lick him until his fur stood up in peaks. She came into heat and howled all night outside. When we got her in the house, she pestered both Willie and Lyle to mate with her which they did much to our amazement as they were two neutered males. After that we got her fixed, but she continued to romance Willie thus earning the nickname "Beanus." She started picking fights with Lyle, terrible fights in the backyard. Willie would stand by and cry, obviously asking them to stop. Poor Bea came to a tragic end. Our next door neighbors had a habit of leaving their garage door halfway down during the day. One day she came over to tell us that our cat was dead, Bea had gotten squished in the garage door. For a long time afterward, we would feel a cat jumping up on the bed at night and settling down between us. No cat was there, and Dave and I were convinced that it was the ghost of Beanus visiting us.

Margaret died of old age at 21, then we lost Bea, then Lyle. We don't know what happened to Lyle and Dave still agonizes over it. Lyle had been sick, vomiting several times a day. The vet gave us medication for it but he wasn't getting better. Then one night Dave swears he went downstairs to let Lyle in late and went back to bed, but in the morning, Lyle was nowhere to be found. Cats have been known to go off by themselves when they die and we think maybe that's what Lyle did. We'll never know for sure. We decided to get a kitten for Willie so we adopted a very young striped tabby kitten from a woman I knew at the credit union where I worked and we named him Junior. He was adorable. I loved that kitten. He was frisky and fun, full of joy at just being alive. I wrote in my journal in August 2008: Life is a circus with Junior around. Willie is slowly making friends with him. He's been so polite and patient, what a lovely cat that Wool is. Junior has been keeping me company while I work and what a little clown. He can climb the chicken wire fence and balance on top. He's a very creative player – always busy.

Junior got a small packrat this afternoon. It got away from him and there he was, crying at the wall of the stairwell outside....the rat had run all the way up the stucco to the roof and there was a jay sitting at the top. Junior was so upset. The jays have been dogging him for weeks now. . He's into killing birds now, unfortunately, got the female woodpecker the other day and now the male has taken off, don't blame him. I hope Jr. takes after Willie and stops after a while. It seems that Willie has gained some 'ethical maturity' about it – he knows we don't like it – or maybe he just got bored with it, who knows?

Willie and Junior are flaked out on the bed upstairs, with Junior cuddling up to Willie's back. He must have had some wild experience outside this morning. Wish we could rig a mini cam to his head and see for ourselves. Would probably scare the hell out of us.

Tuesday, March 25, 2008

We lost Junior last night – I am so sad and upset, I feel like the light has gone out of my life. I called them both in for their dinner around 6:00 and they both came running from outside. Junior ran right in while Willie hung back. I held the screen door open for him and Junior ran out again and into the salt cedar to sharpen his claws. I thought I'd just let them stay outside a little longer. I never saw Junior again. I went outside with the flashlight to search for him around 10:00 and no Junior. This is really really hard....I was just telling Dave that it was going to be so much fun to see Junior enjoy his first spring, but that is not to be. And today, I got an email from the Signpost that they're going to run his picture in their May issue. I had lunch yesterday with Nancy, Kathy and Jo Ann for my birthday and showed them pictures of Es and Junior. Little did I know...

Tuesday evening

The last hope is gone – that he got trapped in our neighbor's garage. He's gone and I'm so sad.

Remembering Junior:

His Ricky Nelson eyes so loving and sweet, like when I came home from Duluth last time.

His long monkey tail with the forward tilting tip. He was so long and slinky I think of him as Rikki Tikki Tavi....with his beautiful stripes and spotted belly and black paw pads.

The way he would run around in the big cottonwood tree like a squirrel, just skylarking.

The way he would sashay in front of you then "salaam" stretching out in the front, then the back until his back legs were stretched out flat, then he would collapse on his side to be petted giving up one of his smiles.

The perfectly round spot on the roof of his mouth that you could see when he yawned.

The way he would slither off the back of the sofa to flop down heavily between Dave and me on the sofa and snuggle in - then slither off the cushions onto the floor.

The way he would lick Willie's face and ears

The way he would tussle with his little white bear up in the bedroom and then carry it downstairs holding it up high in his mouth to play with it in the living room. He would tussle with our hands too and never put out a claw, never scratched

The way he would race and bound over bushes in the back yard, climb the fence and weave in and out of the tomato cages - all the funny things he would do to entertain me when I was working in the garden

I'm going to miss him so much!

Friday, Ma rch 28, 2008

No Junior. I posted two notices with his picture but nothing. I feel like I have a hole in my heart and all the joy has leaked out. Last night Willie cried to get in the bedroom in the middle of the night – Dave heard him –he let him in and Willie got into bed and snuggled tight up against me the rest of the night. Dave said he thinks Willie was trying to comfort me – and himself too. And then I felt a small sad body snuggling up against my back in the very early morning. Am I hallucinating? Maybe so – but Dave and I both on several occasions have felt Bea jump onto our bed and clump up in her way to lay down between us.

Wednesday, April 02, 2008

I had the most wonderful dream last night. A strange man/moth with big round eyes like a cat saw me standing on the bank of a rushing river with a group of people and came up to me – he was holding a strange baby against his chest – and he put his arms around me in a way that was both sexual and reverential, very wonderful. He loved me! He gave me a shopping bag full of rolled up papers to take with me across the river and said he would find me later. When I looked into the bag of grayish documents, there was one packet that was glowing green. I started to take them out to look at them and suddenly the dream was over. What does it mean? I don't know but I do know it made me feel wonderful, something my real life has sure not been doing lately. I noticed too that my grief about Junior has lessened a lot today.

In May I started looking for another striped tabby. I knew I couldn't really replace Junior – every cat is an individual. I found out I could look up cats up for adoption at city shelters online. And that's where I found Junie ten years ago now. Here's from my journal:

Friday, April 11, 2008

I brought the new kitty home from the animal shelter that day – we're calling him Ricky and he's so much like Junior, I think they must be related. I saw his photo online and just had to go see him the next day. When I found his cage, he calmly came to the door and put his paws through to gently play with my fingers. Black paw pads and no claws out – just like Junior. He had me right there! He's long and slinky with a big fat long tail and very vocal and very affectionate. He and Willie have been talking and talking. Willie is fascinated but mad at us, I think. Funny thing – Ricky does not play. He doesn't seem to know how. We'd love to know what his story is – probably a deprived apartment cat. He told his story in cat talk the first night very eloquently and it sounded pretty sad. We think he's missing someone. He's not Junior, he doesn't have the energy and joy that the Jun had, but he's a darn nice cat.

Saturday, April 12, 2008

He and Willie are calm and beginning to play together. When I woke up this morning, June (I want to call him that!) was lying next to me under the covers with his head on the pillow and when I opened my eyes, he patted my cheek with his paw. What a love ! I'm thinking he may be Junior's brother. There was another male cat – Kim told me that Junior was the runt of the litter but had the most personality. She also told me that Junior's mother was very talkative and this new guy sure is.

Friday, April 18, 2008

June is really sick with a cold, a herpes virus. We're giving him amoxy drops anyway even though it's viral. Spent two hours in the car on Tuesday at Dr. Abernathy's waiting my turn. Wasn't bad since I had a good book to read: T. C. Boyle's Drop City. Finally, Dr. A. himself came out to the car – didn't even want him in the clinic – and said that all the animals coming out of that shelter are sick. June's sneezing like crazy and eyes are all watery. He told me that June is closer to a year old than seven months – which supports my suspicion that he is Junior's brother. Unfortunately, the only way I can find out is to tell Kim M. that Junior has disappeared and I don't want to do that. She could find out if the people she gave June to gave him up at the shelter.

Willie now has the cold….curled up in a ball on the sofa in the sunny room. Sneezing non-stop when he's awake…no sneezing when he's asleep.

Sunday, April 20, 2008

Bad day Saturday…for a while I was wondering if June was going to make it – he was so dehydrated. I got him to drink tuna can juice though and he came around a bit. Willie is very sick breathing out of his mouth. Dave got him some Sudafed with pseudoephedrine and I think that's working. I sent an email to the animal shelter ombudsman to complain. (a few days later saw a news item on TV about a kitten dying at the shelter and them quarantining the kittens)…

Thursday, April 24, 2008

On the evening news tonight: a kitten died at the Westside Animal Shelter today and they've quarantined the cats. Huh….our kitties are slowly recovering. I let June outside yesterday and shadowed him the whole time. He had a ball in his quiet way, really loves climbing the salt cedar like a jungle jim. He has stars in his eyes. He especially likes watching TV slumped next to me with a paw on my thigh. He's a house cat for sure

Friday, May 2, 2008

I took June outside this a.m. and he ran all around the cottonwood and the salt cedar, at one point hanging by both front paws from the highest branch. I caught him to break his fall and I think he appreciated it. Nice to see him getting to be a cat and not a couch potato.

Next Day

The June Security Detail got more complicated today – he's learned how to slide the screen door over and get out. Caught him bounding joyfully out the back door this a.m. I've been really diligent about keeping an eye on him outside and I must say it's been nice. I can't multitask though, it's too stressful so I sort of lounge around off on the side while he explores the backyard. He's having a ball and that's very nice to see. Yesterday, he must have spent half an hour draped over a big rock watching the ants and occasionally gently touching one (I think he got bit at one point). He narrowed his eyes down to little pinholes to watch the ants. Very cute. He does all the same things Junior did outdoors: running around in the trees like a squirrel, carrying "prey" high in his mouth and taking it to the side yard to play with, lounging under the same chamisa bushes that Junior liked, among many things. He's a very busy guy just like Jr

June gave me a real workout this a.m. He ran off down the steep hillside to the west into the arroyo chasing a quail and then disappeared. I scrambled down the cliff with Willie following. When we got to the bottom, no June. Willie was calling him but no June so we climbed back up to the top and there's the little stinker in the yard looking all innocent.

May 8, 2008

June found Margaret's wheelchair ramp today and got up on the roof. I had a heck of a time getting him down. He finally got on the tin roof and slid off and fell about 8 feet. I think he's fine though.

And so it went. I gradually relaxed the security patrol as Junie aka Junifer developed street smarts over the years. Sometimes I'll open the door for him to go out and he'll stop to sniff the air then decide not to go out, turn around and come back in. I trust his judgment. I've been criticized for allowing my cats to go outside by people who keep their cats in all the time for fear that a predator will get them. These same cats are flabby grumpy sour creatures. There's certainly a risk, even a big risk, in allowing the cats to go out but the reward is a happy cat who enjoys his life. I think it's morally wrong to hold your cat hostage to your own fears. This was also my parenting philosophy and our daughter now a wife, mother and university teacher is a testament to that philosophy. I don't think she totally appreciates it but she is a very successful adult. Taking risks is "invinegarating" as my husband Dave would say. He built an escape route on all sides of the house, like Margaret's wheelchair ramp, to ensure a quick escape and he showed the cats how to use it.

Streaky was the next cat to enter our lives. He showed up on our roof one day and hung around looking thinner and more bedraggled every day, a homeless cat. We couldn't get near him although he made friends with Willie and June outside. He was unneutered and had a filthy red coat. We felt so bad for him one winter morning seeing him crouched on the windowsill covered in snow. Dave felt so bad for him that he built him a shelter on the roof. Then I saw a flyer with a picture that matched our guy "Lost Cat Streaky....Our Son is Heartbroken." I called the number and talked to the dad who told me that Streaky 'didn't want to live with them anymore,' that he wouldn't come in the house. He said their neighbor lady was putting out food for him and he showed up now and then. He said his son had accepted the fact. I started putting out food for him and very slowly over the next few months he would let us touch him until finally he came in the house. He was terrified of everything, esp. the broom and seemed to have a slight dysplasia in his rear end. The picture was becoming clear about his background and we were very proud of Streaky for having the courage to leave an abusive home to find us. Dave got a trap from the Humane Society to take him in for shots and neutering. This was the real test. Would he stick around after that ? He did, and now spends his evenings between us on the sofa watching TV and sleeping with us at night. I don't think I've ever known a more affectionate and gentle cat. But he also has a passionate and jealous nature to match his red fur, he's like a pit bull of a cat, and I think would rather be an only cat. He got along well with both Willie and June while Willie was alive. Sadly, Will died of old age at 21 at just about the time that Streaky came into the house. Willie was the peacemaker as ever; I never saw him fight with another cat. June and Streaky are not so compatible. Junie at 10 years old is a mature dignified cat who hates being jumped on by a boisterous youngster like Streak. Still, I've seen signs of rapprochement at feeding time. Streaky will lick Junie around the face and ears, but when Junie tries to lick Streaky back, it turns into a boxing match. What's going on? I think it's slowly getting better. They're both in the bed with us in the morning, Junie stretched out between us and Streaky purring and kissing Dave's beard and it's a peaceful lovely time of the day. Dave and I think that Streaky just wants to play and Junie is just too uptight. We need a kitty couples therapist to sort this out......

So that's my life with cats so far...... it would be nice to have one more kitten before I slip my moorings and head out to sea.

Willie and Junie

Streaky the red guy

Dave and I with Willie and June

Dave's favorite cat Willie

Willie and June snoozing

Minnie, the mother of 120 kittens

Junie in the drain

CHAPTER 13

Remembering Junie

We lost our beloved Junie (a boy named June) last Friday to liver disease. He was 15 years old and we'd had him since he was a kitten. My husband Dave is especially grief stricken since June was his companion every morning while Dave drank coffee and watched the sun rise. Junie had his own chair opposite Dave's and would join him while Dave worked on his computer. He was a sweet and gentle tabby cat who had been bullied by our other cat Streaky in recent years. We did our best to protect him and we feel guilty that the stress of the constant attacks contributed to June's illness. Streaky is an aggressive ginger cat who adopted us half a dozen years ago. He had run away from a bad home and hung around outside the house getting thinner and more bedraggled every day until we took him in. The clincher was seeing him on the window sill outside our bedroom covered in snow one morning. At first he got along well with our other two cats but when the peacemaker Willie died of old age at 21, the dynamic changed and he began to bully the remaining cat Junie. We should have 'rehomed' Streak at that point but Dave thought it would break his heart. He was bonded to us and we did admire his courage in leaving his old home and finding us. For a cat he is amazingly obedient. Every time we caught him going after Junie, we'd holler "OUT" and he'd run to the door for a time out.

But enough about Streaky, this is a memoir about Junie.....

I got Junie in May 2007 from the Abq animal shelter. I wanted a cat just like Junior whom we had lost to a predator. I searched online and found a tabby who looked very much like Junior and about the same age, seven months. I got his cage number at the shelter and when I found him, he greeted me by putting his paw through the wire to touch my hand. That was it. I came back the next day to pick him up, the poor guy had to be neutered and vaccinated before I could take him home. I let him out of the pet carrier for the ride home and he lay across my lap like he was exhausted. I think he knew he had found his 'forever home'. I took him to the back bedroom and let him out of the carrier to find his way to Willie in the front of the house. Then the most amazing thing happened: Under the dining room table June talked to Willie for a long time telling his story and Willie listened sympathetically. It sounded like a foreign language in the variety of sounds he made. At times I thought it was getting aggressive but then it turned all soulful and sad. There was one tiny incident that night when Willie ritually trounced Junie for a second or two - and after that they were best friends forever.

Junie was an unusual cat. He was dignified and would not sit on your lap but would lie at your feet like a dog. We wondered what his kittenhood was like and if he had been 'raised' by a dog. One day, a friend visited with his black lab who came to the front door and looked through the glass. June saw him and got all excited and ran to the door only to discover that it was not his Lab and he was visibly disappointed and downcast. He loved the little girls Esme and Silvi and when they visited, he was right there in the middle of them allowing himself to be tugged and tussled and dressed up in doll clothes. Once when they visited we planned a trip to Taos. We were all ready to go, the suitcases in the trunk and no Junie. We looked everywhere for him, we couldn't leave until we found him. We were ready to give up when we looked in the car's trunk and there he was with the suitcases. He was coming along ! (not)

The picture that emerged was a kitten who lived indoors with a dog and small children. He was thrilled with the outdoors but cautious; he never went out of sight of the house. He played on the salt cedar like it was a jungle gym and once I saw him draped over a big rock watching the ants with his eyes narrowed like pinpoints. He figured out how to open all the doors including the sliding screen door. The swinging screen door he opened by jumping up and pushing it open then running through. The inside doors he opened by sticking his paw through and pulling the door towards him. Streak and Willie watched him do this over and over but never learned to do it themselves.

Junie had a thing for snakes, another unusual trait for a cat. We saw him several times chasing and tussling bull snakes but one day, he carried in a rattler and dropped it on the floor in the dining room. He had broken its neck and it could still wriggle but not go anywhere. We let it play out and he ended up eating it under the dining room table. Good eatin'....I've tried rattlesnake myself and it is tasty, like what else....chicken!

Junie began losing weight about a year ago. His behavior changed – on two occasions he bit both Dave and me hard drawing blood. We took him to the vet and the blood draw revealed both thyroid and liver disease. We had to give him three pills a day. Anyone who's ever given a cat a pill knows how daunting this can be. That night, I looked at him down on the floor looking up at me plaintively and I decided to try something different from wrestling with him. I picked him up and put him on the kitchen island, I pulled him in close to my chest while talking softly and sweetly to him. In a few minutes, he melted and opened his mouth to let me give him the pill with the pill popper. I guess the poor guy was starved for affection because he never fought the pill again using the love approach, in fact he would come around looking for us when it was pill time. Dave took over most of the pill duty when he saw how well this worked. June's thyroid got better but not his liver. He got thinner and thinner even though we were feeding him on demand multiple times a day. The vet told us to prepare for the end. That morning came not long after when Dave let him out and found him later curled up under a bush outside. This is what cats do....they hide themselves away and wait for death. Dave brought him in and June went to the bathroom and lay down behind the toilet, something he'd never done before. Dave brought in cushions so we could take turns on the floor being with him and soothing him. I called the vet and we took him in that afternoon to be put to sleep. We brought his body home and laid him out on the living room rug so Streaky could say good-bye then Dave buried him out front near Willie and Margaret and Beanus. We miss him.....Every cat we've had was a unique personality. And now we have Streaky and we think he really loves being the only cat. He talks constantly and follows Dave around all day. He's a total housecat. We'd like to get another kitten but we'll have to see if Streaky will accept him....

Junie and I having a wee kip

Esme and Silvi playing with Junie

Esme and Silvi playing dress up with Junie

Aunt Winnie, Avesa and me in Bermuda circa 2000

CHAPTER 14

Remembering Aunt Winnie

My favorite aunt Winnie died the other day, the day before my 76th birthday. She was 88 years old or thereabouts and her heart, her kind, big old heart, just gave out it seems. Two of her children were with her at the end and I sorely regret that I had not called her the week before as I intended, but thought I'd call this week coming up to thank her for the birthday card she never forgot to send me every year signed by her and Patrick, her youngest son who lived with her and cared for her. What a difference a few days makes. Now I will never hear her voice or her laughter again. I will miss her. She has been a constant in the background of my life since I was a little kid. We kept in touch over the years as we both got on with our lives. I knew her best when we all lived together at Gammy and Gampy's house in Prospect Park, Pa. All but one of their seven children lived with them for a time in the early 50s. The only one absent was Eddie who was in the Air Force in Korea. All the sisters baked him cookies and sent care packages. Elizabeth the oldest sister was there with her husband Ed, their toddler daughter Cathy and baby Nora whom they had adopted in Germany after the war. Second eldest Doris was there with her husband Bus and son, Chuck, a year older than me at five. Then there was my mom Tibby and my dad Don with me and my little sister Pat, who was three, one year younger than me. Ginny and Winnie were teens then followed by the youngest, George. I don't know how we all fit into that house but we did. Gammy made dinner for everyone every night and Ginny and Winnie washed all those dishes. I thought Gammy was a magical cook, her food was delicious. She spent Sunday afternoons making apple pies and dumplings. Ginny and Winnie were very kind to us kids. Once Pat and I decided that the canned goods would look so pretty all silver so we peeled off the labels on a whole shelf of the cabinet. We didn't realize they wouldn't be able to tell what was in the cans. Winnie and Gin took it well, asked us why we did it and just sort of chuckled and didn't punish us. Looking back, I realize how lucky we didn't get a whupping for that. This was the 50s after all and kids were whipped and spanked all the time for less than that. I remember Gammy getting mad at Georgie and saying "go pick me a switch" off the peach tree. George would disappear for the rest of the day. Maybe that was her intention but when he showed up for dinner, it was all forgotten.

My favorite memory of Aunt Winnie was the time she took me, just me, on the bus to Chester for an afternoon of shopping when I five. It was the biggest adventure I had ever had. I saw my first black person on the bus and I'm afraid I shouted in my excitement "look, Aunt Winnie, it's a chocolate man!!" She shushed me but I noticed people either smiling or frowning at me and the poor black man looked both a little frightened and a little amused. I kept trying to catch his eye to smile at him and he did once a little bit. It was confusing. This was the Jim Crow era so now I understand why. Aunt Winnie and I arrived in Chester and had a great time shopping. I stuffed my pockets with toys from the five and dime. Only later that night when I showed my parents the toys did I find out there was this thing called money and you had to pay for things with money. This was a groundbreaking day for me. Aunt Win said she was not aware of the shoplifting. We had a great lunch at the Woolworth counter, a hot dog and milkshake. It was heaven.

Winnie left high school not long after and got a typist job. There she met and fell in love with Jim "Chief" Mitchell who would become her husband of 50 plus years and the father of her four children: Jimmer, Doris, Sue and Patrick. I was a flower girl at their wedding, such a glamorous and romantic event with a reception at the VFW Hall afterwards I remember the splintery dance floor and the roast beef sandwiches and sips of Rolling Rock beer....we watched Winnie and Jim dance their first dance as a married couple. They looked like they were so madly in love.

She left us then and moved to Petaluma, California where Jimmer was born. Chief was stationed in Labrador for a while and Winnie and the baby came home to stay with her parents. This is when we saw another side of Winnie. We were playing in the yard next to Gammy's house with a bunch of kids, one a bully. We were taking turns on the hammock swinging it hard. The bully wouldn't give up his turn so we swung him extra hard until the hammock flipped over and he was trapped in it. His fly must have been open because we saw his dingle dangling down from the netting in the hammock. We laughed and howled, ran next door to tell Aunt Winnie about it. We were shocked because rather than laugh, she gave us a severe lecture. I thought at the time whoa that was what getting married and having a baby must do to you..

They lived in a lot of places after that wherever Chief was stationed in the Air Force. I think Okinawa was her favorite. They were assigned to Nellis AFB in Las Vegas and that's where they settled after he retired. I visited them several times there and remember good times talking around the kitchen table.

Aunt Winnie was the traditional housewife raising four kids and running the household. She never smoked or drank and went to Jazzercise every week into her 80s. She kept in touch with friends and family and told them she loved them whenever she talked to them. She was a practicing Catholic who attended Mass on Sunday. She was about as straight as they come. She was always close to Aunt Ginny who moved to Vegas to be near her. Ginny often called her by her baby name "Wee." Gammy lived with Win for a while after Gampy's death in the late 70s followed by Tibby and Ginny in their old age for a time. They are all gone now. George is the last Gilpin standing of the seven siblings.

Aunt Winnie was a generous, loving and kind person who will be greatly missed by those of us who are still here. She was the heart of the family. Among her siblings, she was the favorite and the one everyone trusted and knew they could count on. She was the best.

George and Winnie, 1945.

Snowy day in our backyard in Placitas

CHAPTER 15

Weather Report

*T*he weather in the Land of Enchantment is endlessly varied and dramatic. Here are some observations of weather and wildlife during a winter and early spring in Placitas, New Mexico, a village on the northern foothills of the Sandia Mountains

Sunday, January 11, 2004

Went for a walk in the Open Space this morning. The land is brown talcum ready to blow away in the spring winds. But the land is patient, it knows how to wait. When the rain does return—this drought can't last forever—the land will come alive from dormant seeds and roots that go deep. It will be amazing and miraculous.

January 25, 2004

Big dramatic weather day. As I walked down the road I could see across the tawny hills covered with juniper trees like dotted swiss over the river valley and onto the high white Jemez Mountains with their deep-cut mysterious canyons. Snowstorms seethed in the canyons spinning off the tops while big gray cumulus clouds raced across the valley. It was exhilarating. Looking at those vast distant mountains, I flashed on a chipmunk family (or do they live alone?) snoozing in their furry leafy den between the twisted roots one of those huge vanilla-scented pine trees.

January 26, 2004

Icy wind skittered past my cheeks like razors this morning on my walk. Even our hot sun burning in a deep blue sky didn't do much to warm things up. Icy tatters of snow from yesterday's snowstorm were flung across the homely brown rocks like old lace. I busted thick ice out of the bird bath (we jokingly call our backyard bird station, "The Rockwell Bird n' Bunny Spa.") and poured in a big bucket of hot hot water for the robins and bluebirds. It does my heart good to see them out there, sometimes six robins at a time, sipping away like they're at a tea party.

January 27, 2004

The sun is warming up the bare hills, and they are like loaves of bread rising ever so slightly. Some snow still glistens on the north slopes. A foxy little girl coyote crossed the arroyo ahead of me and ran up the slope. She paused at the top and we looked at one another for a half a minute. A close look at a coyote dispels any notion that they are wild dogs. They are quite a different animal, with their triangular pointy faces and fat rumpy tail. Last year, I surprised an old grizzled male in a deep arroyo north of home. He scooted ahead, then turned to look at me over his muscular shoulder. He had my father's eyes. We stared into one another's eyes for what seemed like a long time and then he was gone.

January 28, 2004

Beautiful, cold, clear, blue and silver winter day. I turned my compost pile, a chore that I always drag myself to do then thoroughly enjoy. The pile is cooking nicely despite the cold weather: all the garbage is breaking down into lovely crumbly brown stuff, food for the garden. I'm always fascinated by the decomposing process, the fermenting energy of last week's wilted broccoli, potato peels, egg shells and coffee grinds worked over by legions of pill bugs and worms, turning into pure gold for the garden. I've tried to convey my sense of joy and pride in my compost pile to others and they look at me like I'm a little nuts. Only another gardener could understand.

January 29, 2004

Another beautiful, still, crystalline winter day. A dewy blue mist lit up by a golden light lay around the tops of the Sandias. A fleet of thin white clouds sailed off the tops to the southwest.

January 30, 2004

The Sandias were in shadow with gleaming snow filtering down through the steep craggy slopes; the sky overhead so blue it's almost purple. The Jemez are tinged with a phlegm yellow haze from the City's rotten lungs. It's time for some rain and wind to wash it way. I hang out the whites and darks, one of life's great pleasures for me..

January 31, 2004

The cleansing storm is on the way. Snow is predicted for later today and into tomorrow. Hooray! Great gray clouds hang over the Jemez, their bulging bellies grazing the peaks. The light this morning is flat and ugly, makes you realize how much the light contributes to the beauty of this place. It's all about the light.

February 1, 2004

Woke up to a sunny snowy winter landscape. A gusty wind sent showers of glittering snowflakes swirling off the roof. Towering, deep-bellied snow clouds still hung over the Jemez, dumping snow as though through a funnel into the abysmal canyons below Redondo Peak.

February 7, 2004

Pure blue skies, icy air that tingles the nostril hairs and invigorates the getting-sick lungs. The horses, just turned out, whirl around and kick at one another. Off in the Open Space coyote howls skirled like banshees. Wonder why...are they fighting over some torn-apart rabbit or do they just feel good in this crispy air? Turns out this is the beginning of their mating season.

The last patches of snow are glazed ice and sparkle like diamonds as I pass by.

February 9, 2004

Frigid blue sky day - yet - on the kitchen window a delicate pale green lacewing clung to the glass. She looked miserable and cold, longing towards the garden. Where did she come from in the dead of winter? She must have hatched from garden soil in one of the pots in the sunroom. Why didn't she stay in that sunny room? She must be drawn to the garden where her mother laid her eggs on a hot summer day - or was it a warm fall day?. I've seen lacewings into October. So many mysteries. I coaxed her onto a matchbook cover - she's so fragile, my fingers would've crushed her no matter how gentle I was - and put her on the big oxalis in the sunroom. She immediately disappeared into the stems to live out her short life - or is it a long life?

February 11, 2004

Whitish glary high thins, ugly day, snow later they say. As I hung out the sheets, I listened in on two finches having a conversation high up in the cottonwood tree. They must be mates: he has a bright red chest and she has a striped brown and white chest. They're always together. I see them at my window feeder all day as I work at the computer. Their conversation went on and on, back and forth, not singing, but talking in their little waxy voices, endlessly varied. I could have been listening to a conversation in Portuguese or Greek. I wonder what they talk about....
This cold is hanging on. I can't seem to warm up, no wonder it's called a cold! Yesterday, I lay down on the cushy pink rug in the sun and after a few minutes, I felt a tiny tap on my shoulder. Rolling over, there was Willy who then flopped down next to me and stretched out full length. What a luxurious animal.

February 12, 2004

Big blizzard raged all night and through the morning. The wind screamed and howled all night. The snow is piled up high in drifts in some places and swept bare in others. I followed my old farmers habit, the animals eat first, and went out to fill the bird water and feeders before coffee and toast. It used to be a lot more work when we had the horses and chickens. Other than that, I'm staying in. Willy is still up in our bed this late morning, cuddled up under the covers.

February 13, 2004

Bitter bitter cold today. The sun came out for a few hours yesterday afternoon and in a short time melted all but the north-facing snow. This morning the sun was muffled behind flung-out fleecy clouds just in the eastern part of the sky; the rest of the sky is clear so it will warm up today. I just let Willy in, and he was covered with dirt and leaves. I took him into the garage and used an old horse brush to clean him off. He let me hold him up under the armpits with my forearm against my body as I brushed off his belly. He stretched out to about three feet long and went totally limp. What a character.

Monday, February 16, 2004

Presidents Day today, a lovely holiday, and the 8th anniversary of our moving to this beautiful place. The junipers are turning that ominous orange color. Any day now they'll begin spewing out their pollen like smoke, and we'll be popping the allergy pills. Spring is just around the corner. The sky is a luminous blue today; the sun is pouring down like honey. Time to get out in the garden to clear out last summer's dead vines.

Tuesday, February 17, 2004

A fine haze like the sheerest chiffon covers the sky, matching my melancholy mood. The blue still shows through but the light is like an old fashioned sepia print. There seems to be a hush over everything, it's very very quiet this morning, like the calm before a storm.

Wednesday, February 18, 2004

Another hazy day beginning with a blue sky strewn with long, thin clouds curling up on the ends like fiddler ferns, their beauty marred by dozens of jet contrails, probably dribbling jet fuel over the landscape. Ranchera music blared from the home construction site down the hill reeking of roof tar and off in the distance a car alarm shrieked. There's so much about the modern world that I hate, and these are just a few of my favorites

Friday, February 20, 2004

Pewter gray sky, completely windless and still, storms on the way this weekend.

Saturday, February 21, 2004

It's spitting rain and promises to rain for the next three days. Hooray !! The air is moist and fresh, heavy trundling pregnant clouds have settled into the lower canyons of the Jemez and Sandias, making a landscape that reminds me of ancient Chinese art like Travelers among Mountains and Streams.

Sunday, February 22, 2004

Dave all excited called me out this morning to see a frost that he says he's seen only a few times in his life. On top of the cars, early morning, was a patina of frost that looked like the endpapers on fine books. The air was so fresh after the rain yesterday it smelled like pine...and more rain on the way this week. The cats wandered around outside for hours sniffing everything and searching out tender blades of new grass to chew on.

Saturday, February 28, 2004

Heavy snow and high winds last night. As we approach noon though, it's melting off rapidly. We are going to have a GREAT wildflower season this year after all this snow. There was another 18" on top of the Sandias last night. My favorite little bird, the titmouse, just landed on the window feeder. Adorable with his perky little pointy cap and shiny round black eyes. Obviously intelligent the way he looks you over. I love the way they eat a seed: they grab a sunflower seed out of the feeder and fly to a nearby tree limb, throw the seed under their feet and tap away at it until it's broken open to eat. Then back for another one

Sunday, February 29, 2004

Dramatic violent weather day. Academy Award weather performance. One after the other, huge storms build up over the Jemez and sweep across the valley, engulfing the house in snow and just as quickly sweep away, revealing an intensely blue sky with schooners of white clouds sailing by, golden light contrasted with deep shadows on the ground.

Tuesday, March 2, 2004

Stepped up to the kitchen sink and just outside the window was a roadrunner as big as a Rhode Island Red. He (she?) was in full feather - it's cold, windy and gray today, another storm on the way. He stared at me with those crazy eyes that twirl like pinwheels and raised and lowered his black crest several times, then turned and glided off. I'd think he's totally comical, a Groucho Marx of a bird, except that I know what a stone cold killer he is to everything in his path, including the little finches. He's a velociraptor in a clown suit. I got to know their ways when we lived in Corrales for almost 20 years. There were lots more roadrunners there than here in Placitas where they are rarely seen. The cats were afraid of them. I remember seeing a roadrunner stop dead upon seeing a garden hose loosely coiled on the ground. He went into a crouch then charged the hose and pounced on the brass fitting at the end and lifted and shook it, only then realizing his mistake. I thought what an incredible ego to think he could tackle a snake that size !

Saturday, March 6, 2004

Windy cold blue day. The snow is streaming off the tops of the Sandias like white smoke. We'll go Tuesday to xc up there; it would be miserable today with the wind. The Sandias do look gorgeous from here though - dazzling white from top to bottom against a deep blue sky. Looks like the Hindu Kush. The ground is saturated after all the rain and snow. Are we going to have an explosion of flowers !!

Sunday, March 7, 2004

After some tentative beginnings, slapped down by big storms, Spring is finally making some headway today. It is GORGEOUS today. I sat out on the steel chair by our campfire and enjoyed the warm sun and gentle breezes. Willy sat on my lap for awhile then rolled around on the ground in kitty ecstasy, covering himself with leaves and dirt.

Our backyard in winter

Looking out to the Jemez Mountains

Storm coming our way

Big weather drama as seen from our porch

The bench out on our point

On the path to the point on our ridge

References

The North American Philadelphia, Sunday, May 24, 1908, Page 1"The Philadelphia of Our Ancestors -- Old Philadelphia Families" by Frank W Leach, 1908

History of Chester County, Pennsylvania, with Genealogical and Biographical Sketches, Volume 2,by J. Smith Futhey and Gilbert Cope, Republished by Heritage Books, MD 2007; Originally published by Louis H Everts, Philadelphia, 1881

Quaker Date Book 1961

"The Gilpin Family" J. Painter. Lima, Pa.1870 Albert Cook Myers R. L. Cooke, Jr. R. L. Cooke, III Bob CookeWikipedia

"A Study of Delaware Indian Medicine Practice and Folk Beliefs" by Gladys Tantawquidgeon, Pennsylvania Historical Commission, 1942

Colonial and Revolutionary Families of Pennsylvania by John W. Jordan, Genealogical Publishing Com. 2004

"Indians of New Jersey, Dickon Among the Lenapes" M.R. Harrington, Rutgers University Press, 1963

About the Author

Barbara Rockwell is happily retired, a reluctant activist, library volunteer, cook and grandmother. She is the author of Boiling Frogs, Intel vs. the Village. She lives in Placitas, New Mexico with her husband of 45 years.

Other Works

BOILING FROGS: INTEL VS. THE VILLAGE

The story goes that if you throw a frog into a pot of boiling water, he will jump out and save himself. If you place the same frog in a pot of cool water and slowly bring it to a boil, he will allow himself to be boiled to death. This is exactly what is happening to millions of people around the world. Industry has introduced tens of thousands of chemical compounds into our human environment since World War II. We are the frogs in a vast scientific experiment.

In 1992, Intel Corporation tightened its grip on the mesa above the village of Corrales, New Mexico, building its two-billion-dollar flagship plant there. Soon the battle is on between the unholy triad of big money, big business, and politics and a band of "quaint guerillas" that see their peaceful rural lifestyle threatened by the new neighbor on the hill. Touted as a "clean industry," residents soon find out that making computer chips is anything but clean, as tons of toxic chemicals pollute the air they breathe, and their water is pumped out from under them at an alarming rate. Boiling Frogs is a shocking tell-all, a fully documented report of Intel's takeover of New Mexico, and a cautionary tale for anyone who wakes up to find out that a corporate monster has moved in next door.

Made in the USA
Monee, IL
02 December 2022

19038099R00163